GOLDA MEIR SPEAKS OUT

GOLDA MEIR
SPEAKS OUT

Edited by Marie Syrkin

Steimatzky's Agency

together with

Weidenfeld and Nicolson

Weidenfeld and Nicolson
5 Winsley Street
London W1

Weidenfeld and Nicolson Jerusalem
19 Herzog Street
Jerusalem

ISBN   0 297 99558 8

Printed and bound in Israel by Keter Press

Contents

6   *Contents*

GOLDA MEIR SPEAKS OUT

Biographical Data

Born Golda Mabovitch on May 3, 1898, in Kiev, Russia, she arrived in the United States in 1906. The family settled in Milwaukee, where she graduated from high school and enrolled in the Milwaukee Normal School. She joined the Socialist-Zionist Poale Zion in 1915. She married Morris Myerson in 1917 and left with him for Palestine in 1921. After several years in the kibbutz of Merhavia she moved to Tel Aviv and later to Jerusalem, where their two children were born.

She rapidly rose to leadership in the young labor movement of Palestine, becoming the head of the Political Department of the Histadrut. When, during the 1940's, in the course of Jewish Palestine's struggle with the mandatory power for the right to bring in Jewish refugees, the British arrested the male leaders of the Jewish community, Mrs. Myerson was chosen acting head of the Political Department of the Jewish Agency in Jerusalem. Moshe Sharett was head of the Political Department of the Jewish Agency. In this capacity she was among those that negotiated with the British till the creation of the state of Israel. Just before the establishment of the state, disguised as an Arab woman, she secretly went to Transjordan for a meeting with King Abdullah to try to persuade him not to join the anticipated attack of the Arab states on Israel.

Upon the establishment of Israel in 1948, she was appointed minister to Moscow. In 1949, after Israel's first elections, Mrs.

9

Myerson, a leading Mapai figure, joined the Cabinet as Minister of Labor. In 1956 she became Foreign Minister; she then Hebraized her name to Meir. She retired from the Foreign Ministry in 1965 and became Secretary of Mapai. In March, 1969, following the death of Prime Minister Levi Eshkol, Mrs. Meir became Prime Minister of Israel.

Foreword

These statements by Golda Meir, in addition to being a powerful exposition of all facets of Israel's case, constitute a kind of oral autobiography in which Mrs. Meir's extraordinary personality is expressed in her own words. Not limited to the years of Mrs. Meir's tenure as Minister of Labor, Foreign Minister, and Prime Minister, they span a lifetime of intense involvement in every aspect of the modern fight for Jewish independence. From the engagingly candid "My Beginnings," a description of her childhood and youth, to the last chapter in this volume, "My Life Has Been Blessed," in which she sums up the totality of her experience as woman and stateswoman, these statements reflect crucial moments in a struggle which began with Mrs. Meir's arrival in the wasteland Palestine of 1921 and has still not ended.

Mrs. Meir's remarkable effectiveness as a speaker springs not only from her natural eloquence, but from the moral authority of her stance. From the outset she was first doer, then exponent. She addresses the Anglo-American Commission of Inquiry as a Socialist labor leader of the Histadrut, Palestine's great trade union. She protests the deportation of the refugees on the SS *Exodus 1947* back to Germany, from the shore of the land the Jewish survivors are seeking to enter. In 1948, as yet comparatively unknown to her audience, she galvanizes a conference of Jewish fund-raising bodies with an unscheduled appearance not only because of her graphic account of the odds against the 600,000 Jews of Palestine, but because she herself has traveled the ambushed roads between Tel Aviv and besieged Jerusalem and has been with Haganah units that lacked blankets and weapons. And when she calls on American Jewry to go on alyah, to "ascend" to Israel, she does so as one who left a promising career in Milwaukee and whose daughter and grandchildren are in a Negev kibbutz.

Since girlhood Mrs. Meir has always been directly engaged in battle, whether against the swamps of her kibbutz or reactionary social concepts in the emerging economy of Palestine, or the betrayal of the "promise" by the mandatory government, or a growing ring of external foes. This enormously active life was embraced despite deep family attachments and at great personal cost. Her early discussion ("Women's Lib—1930") of the problems faced by a woman not satisfied with the traditional roles of wife and mother poignantly reveals the psychic conflict she suffered as a young woman. Nevertheless, at no point was there a real dichotomy between the demands of her personal life and her imperious need to take part to the fullness of her ability in the social and political movements in which she believed. In moments of decision there was little doubt about her choice. One example will suffice. In youth she refused to marry the boy she loved until he agreed to go with her to pioneer in Palestine. Because of this unyielding commitment to her cause, her addresses, for all their variety of subject matter, have an inner harmony and progress dramatically to their climax—the establishment and defense of Israel. The youthful dream, which to all save a dedicated few seemed an illusory spark, blazes into the steady light of her old age.

Many of Mrs. Meir's most moving statements are not the formal addresses at the Knesset or the United Nations but those delivered extemporaneously during some crisis in Israel's struggle for survival. Many of the pieces in this collection fall into this category and, whether delivered in Hebrew, English, or Yiddish, have been rescued from the stenographic records of the meetings at which they were given. Other informal statements in which Mrs. Meir analyzes social problems in pithy, homely terms throw light on her attitudes as labor leader and Socialist. They reflect her unaffected good sense and human sympathy in the most personal sense.

Mrs. Meir's simplicity of style corresponds to the clarity with which she perceives the essentials of a problem. Though opponents may charge "oversimplification," her ability to disengage the kernel of truth from the husk of spurious complexities is a refreshing gift in the midst of diplomatic double-talk. She is never afraid to insist on the obvious if it is important, and in her straightforward fashion she refuses to be deflected by what she considers false or irrelevant no matter how expedient it might be to appear rhetorically more "flexible." Though she can be sharply witty in her rejoinders, she is never seduced into cleverness, and though never ashamed of emotion, she is too genuine to decline into cant. This makes her a formidable antagonist.

The absolute assurance—she is not fashionably hesitant about absolutes or making "value judgments"—with which Mrs. Meir upholds the justice of Israel's position is grounded as much on her own experience as on the tenets of Zionist ideology. She needs no statistics to be certain that the labor of her pioneer generation in the malaria-ridden Emek expropriated no one save the mosquitoes. She knows that the liberated Turkish province to which she came was historic "Palestine" only for the Jewish settlers and merely "Southern Syria" for those Arabs who then had nationalist aspirations. She remembers with what pain the Jewish community accepted the further truncation of the Jewish homeland through the Partition Resolution of 1947 and how desperately she herself pleaded with the Arabs to set up their parallel Palestine state and live in amity with the Jews. Consequently she is wholly free of the selective "guilt complex" evidenced by some young Jews more familiar with Israel's victories than with the realities preceding the founding of the Jewish state.

Although Mrs. Meir has repeatedly expressed sorrow for the deliberately protracted plight of the displaced Arabs, she accepts no blame for their condition. In her view the Arab refugee problem is the result of three concerted Arab attempts to destroy Israel, and it can readily be solved by a true peace. She put it plainly: "I am sorry; I cannot sympathize with the poor Arab states because they failed to exterminate us. The existence and independence of Israel are not negotiable." And if she now insists on "secure and agreed borders" according to the terms of the 1967 Resolution, it is partly because of her bitter memory of her acquiescence, as Foreign Minister, in the withdrawal of Israel from the Sinai and Gaza in 1957, only to have the terms of the agreement promptly broken by Egypt. When critics worry that because of the exigencies of defense, Israel, contrary to its liberal tradition, may become "militaristic," she can bluntly answer: "I don't want a nice, liberal, antimilitaristic, *dead* Israel." On the other hand, she can with equal honesty declare in a much-quoted utterance: "Someday when peace comes, we may forgive the Arabs for having killed our sons, but it will be harder for us to forgive them for having forced us to kill their sons."

Her formal statements on the Arab refugees, the Sinai campaign of 1956, and various aspects of the present confrontation with the Arab states and Soviet Russia provide the historical frame of reference and an authoritative exposition of Israel's side of the controversy, making this collection an invaluable contribution to our knowledge of the Middle East conflict and the emergence of Israel. At the same time it offers an intimate understanding of the dynamic of Zionism as given by its most famous living practitioner. Not least, through Mrs. Meir's own words, we gain an insight into the woman who, without feminist fanfare, has become one of the major figures of her time.

MARIE SYRKIN

1. My Beginnings

From a radio interview given by Mrs. Meir in Israel. (In Hebrew, 1969)

I was born in 1898 in Kiev, a city outside the Jewish Pale of Settlement, after our parents and my sister had moved there from Pinsk, a town deep in the Pale. I lived in Kiev until the age of five and I hardly remember the place—not even the yard in front of the house. However, I have three separate, vivid memories of Kiev. First, the death of my grandmother, Father's mother. (Our youngest sister, the one who remained in America, was born on the same day.)

The second is the rumor that there would be a pogrom in Kiev. It was characteristic of my father that he made no attempt to hide his family. We lived on the first floor. There were stairs in the entry, leading to a neighbor's house on the second floor. I remember standing on the stairs together with a little girl, a neighbor's daughter, of about my own age, and watching my father and the neighbor trying to fortify the entry by nailing boards across the door. Fortunately, no pogrom took place at that time, but the whole town was full of rumors of a forthcoming massacre.

The third thing I remember of our Kiev period is hunger. One picture is engraved in my memory. When my younger sister, four years my junior, was still a baby, six months old or less, my mother was cooking porridge, a great luxury for us in those days. My mother gave me a little and the rest to my baby sister. She finished eating before me; then Mother took a little of my porridge away from me to give her. The dish was one I did not get to eat every day. I remember my shock at being deprived of this rare porridge. From my older sister's stories I know how often she went to school without eating; she would faint from hunger in school.

Before we moved to Kiev, we had lived with my mother's father, Menahem Naiditch, in Pinsk, a town on the Dnieper. A long row of inns lined the road to the river. One of the inns belonged to Grandfather; a few houses further on, close to the Dnieper, was the house of Moshe Sharett's grandfather. Grandfather had a big house, with a big yard, in which the whole family lived, including the married daughters. We had lived with him before we moved to Kiev, but life had been hard even in Pinsk. And Father, who came originally from the Ukraine—he was not born in Pinsk—looked for a way to improve the condition of the family. That's why we moved to Kiev, outside the Pale of Settlement for Jews. Father, a skilled carpenter, belonged to the category of Jews who could get a permit to live outside the Pale. So the family moved to Kiev, where Father got government work.

Father was no ordinary carpenter. His special skill in making beautiful, ornamental furniture won him a contract for its manufacture. Of course, he had to borrow money for this job, and he set up a workshop with a few employees. But in the end—Father always used to say it was anti-Semitism—his furniture was not accepted by the contractor although he was a fine craftsman. And there we were, with many debts and without a penny to live on. Father used to go to work far from home. He would come home at night in the Russian frost and find nothing to eat. If there was salt herring on the table, that was a red-letter day. So when I reached the age of five—my older sister was fourteen and our youngest sister still a baby—we went back to live with Grandfather in Pinsk. By then there already was a plan afoot for Father to go to America to mend the family fortunes.

I never knew my father's father. In those days the czar's government used to snatch Jewish boys of twelve or thirteen—wherever they might be found—for the Russian Army. Grandfather was one of these kidnapped children. He was snatched at the age of thirteen and spent thirteen years in the Russian Army. The authorities tried to make him change his religion; he would be forced to kneel on a patch of ground covered with peas for hours at a time. From family tales I gather that Grandfather was very orthodox. During all the thirteen years he spent in the Russian Army he ate no cooked food because it was not kosher. Even after his release—so Father told us—he feared that despite his abstinence he might have sinned unwittingly. So he slept on a bench in the synagogue for many years, with a stone for a pillow to atone for a sin he had never committed—at least not knowingly. That was Grandfather, as we heard about him from Father, for Grandfather was no longer alive when we were born. He died young.

Of Grandmother, my memory is very dim—all I remember is a very tall, thin woman, who was very strict with us. I suppose that was the result of the kind of life she led. My father too was tall and thin, with delicate features. Unlike his parents, he was not extremely orthodox, but he respected Jewish tradition. Consequently, the atmosphere at home was always traditional, first in Russia, later in America, and finally, when our parents settled here, in Palestine.

We did not go to America together with Father when he left Kiev. He went first while the rest of the family returned to Pinsk. For a while we stayed in Grandfather's house; then we moved to a rented room nearby.

Father was three years in America without us. During those years I did not go to school but had private lessons in arithmetic, reading, and writing. My father, like most immigrants of those days, first went to New York. To get there was far from simple, for he hardly had money for his own journey, and certainly none for the whole family. That was one reason why he left us in Russia, but there was still another. Like many Jews who left Russia for the United States in those days, he did not view his emigration as permanent. Despite czarist oppression, the pull of home was great. His plan was to go to America, the land of infinite opportunities—all you had to do was to get there and become rich straightaway. And then, after a year or two, he would return to the familiar environment of the *stetl*, the intimate Jewish hometown of the Pale, with the riches he had acquired in the United States.

In New York, he got work for the princely wage of three dollars a week. On that he somehow managed to live and also send some of the three dollars to us to help support the family. I don't understand this financial wizardry.

Father and Mother were deeply attached to each other. Contrary to the custom, they had a romantic encounter. In those days marriages were usually arranged by a *shadchan*, a marriage broker; the girl didn't even have to meet the boy; the parents did the choosing. I don't quite understand why Father, born in the Ukraine, had to enlist in the Russian Army in Pinsk. But Mother always used to tell us with great pride that one day she saw a tall, handsome young man on the street and fell in love with him at first sight. When she came home, she boldly confessed her infatuation to Grandfather and Grandmother. The *shadchan* was called in to settle the match after her prodding. Grandfather had many daughters, but Mother was his darling. I don't know if another of his daughters could have convinced Grandfather that she be allowed to marry a young man who had taken her fancy. But Mother managed it. Father was a poor youth whose own father was no longer alive; however, he came from a fairly good family, for at the age of twelve or thirteen he had been sent to the Slonim yeshiva, where he studied in extreme poverty—*essen teg und trinken trehren* . . . ("to eat days and swallow tears"). I suppose you know what this expression means from old stories—many older people here are familiar with this bit of Jewish experience. A young boy from a poor family would be sent to study at some yeshiva. Charitable families would undertake to provide his daily board; his bed would be a bench in the yeshiva. Since very few students were lucky enough to find a family willing and able to feed them for the whole week, they would have to arrange to board each day with a different family. Sometimes the food was good, and sometimes not. A Jewish song of the period describes *essen teg und shlingen trehren*. It tells how the boys "ate days and swallowed tears," because not every mistress of the house welcomed the child who was her boarder, and the food was often bad or scanty. At any rate, by virtue of the yeshiva, Father was no ignoramus. He was an educated young man who knew the Torah. That was chalked up to his credit when he was considered as a suitor; besides, Mother was stubborn and pampered. Apparently Grandmother and Grandfather knew that if she had made up her mind that she wanted this young man, no one else would do.

Mother had eight children, four sons and four daughters. Of these only three daughters survived. The other five children died in infancy, including all the boys. I did not get to know them because they died so young. I think only one of the five lived to the age of two; two children died in one week.

Father and Mother were entirely different types. All his life, Father was very innocent and confiding. He generally trusted a man till he had been proved wrong. Naturally, he had quite a number of misadventures, and we often suffered as a result. But he was unfailingly warmhearted, always ready to do things for others and to see the good in everyone. Mother was beautiful, energetic, shrewd, clever, more realistic than Father and altogether more enterprising. Despite their troubles, both of them were very cheerful, very optimistic.

As I have said, Father was no extremist in religion, but traditionally observant, particularly in Grandfather's house. I remember the festivals and the Friday nights when the whole family would assemble. (We were a very large family, but after the Holocaust not a trace remained of those who had stayed in Pinsk.) There were always guests on Friday night, and all sang the Sabbath hymns. Both Mother and Father had very beautiful voices. To this day my sister's children and my own sing the way Grandfather used to sing. Both my sister's children and my own used to celebrate the holidays in Palestine with

Father and Mother, who arrived here in 1926, a few years after us. For many years our children enjoyed Father's company; they loved their grandfather deeply and remember him.

But let us get back to the days in America. Father worked for a while in New York, and then he was sent out to Milwaukee by Hias, the organization that dealt with Jewish immigrants in those days. One of its aims was to disperse Jewish immigrants and not let them concentrate in New York. Father had never heard of Milwaukee, and nobody asked him his wishes. They simply told him that he would get better work in Milwaukee.

In Pinsk Mother struggled to maintain the family, and Grandfather helped a little. My elder sister, who was fifteen or sixteen at the time, did not go to work; she studied. But her main activity was a dangerous business which caused Mother a great deal of trouble and distress and settled the fate of the family, so that instead of Father's returning to Pinsk, we went to America. My sister had joined a revolutionary movement—true, it was Zionist-Socialist, but this too was forbidden. One of the most terrible recollections I have of those days is of my sister habitually disappearing from the house at the beginning of the evening and coming home very late. We lived near the police station; I—and especially Mother—would hear the dreadful cries of young men and women arrested for illegal activity who were being brutally beaten. I suppose the police wanted to extract the names of their comrades from them, and no doubt the young revolutionaries would not yield.

In those days, Cossacks would periodically come to Pinsk. They would gallop through the town on their horses, not caring on whom they trampled, and would brutally beat any suspected young men or women they might find. At this point Mother started to write to Father that because of my sister's activities we could not remain in Pinsk but must go to America.

My sister had a great, perhaps decisive, influence on my life. On Sabbath, when Mother went to the synagogue, she would conveniently arrange clandestine meetings at home. In the Russia of those times there was generally a big coal stove, on whose top you could lie, built into the wall. As a small child I used to climb onto the stove and listen to the secret discussions of my sister and her friends. I knew that something forbidden was going on. Poor Mother used to come home from the synagogue and realize what was doing in her house. She was afraid a policeman might come and catch the conspirators, so she became a kind of sentry. She would walk up and down beside the house so that if a policeman should approach—to this day I remember the name of the policeman everyone was afraid of, Lassok—she could warn them immediately. Perhaps I understand better today than I did then how much Mother suffered because of my sister's political activities. But my sister inherited a brimming measure of Father's obstinacy, for despite his amiable disposition, he was a very stubborn man.

My sister belonged to the Zionist-Socialist Party; other young Jewish dissidents belonged to the Bund, the large organization of anti-Zionist Jewish workers. I still remember the arguments with the Bundist youth. From the talk I heard as I sat on the stove I knew that we were not Bundists but Socialist-Zionists.

All this activity was illegal, and most parents opposed their children's involvement. Chaim Weizmann's family also lived in Pinsk, but I believe that their attitude was different—perhaps the parents were more liberal. We lived in a room rented from a *shochet*, a kosher slaughterer, a poor man with an only daughter. I remember him well—a tall man with a white beard, highly respected in the city. My fifteen-year-old sister introduced his daughter to evil ways—she brought her into the party. This was a terrible tragedy for her family because the parents naturally wanted to protect their children. Teen-agers who had to transport forbidden publications from one place to another at night or come together in the forest for illegal meetings were in deadly danger, and the parents objected. Mother was different. She did not object because she knew my sister belonged to a Zionist party; however, all parties were illegal, and membership in any political party could endanger liberty and often life.

As I said before, one of my three first memories was the preparations for a pogrom. I don't know what I felt at the time apart from fear. Now, retrospectively, I can interpret it—no doubt there was also an angry feeling of impotence, for what was the use of a few planks across the door? And at home I heard that all the hunger we suffered was due to anti-Semitism; that was why Father's work wasn't accepted and why we were hungry. But I was most influenced by my sister's illegal activities. At any rate, I got my first lesson in illegal activity at that time in Pinsk.

I have another early memory. In Pinsk there was a row of big buildings in the street that led to the bank of the river. Opposite, on a hill, stood a monastery. I was terrified of the unkempt beggars who sat in front of the monastery, praying all the time and begging for charity. When Mother wanted to frighten me, she would talk about these beggars.

From the age of five to eight, we had lived only among Jews in the Pale. I cannot say that I took from Russia anything that later aroused nostalgia. I took with me memories of the Cossacks: on one eve of the Fast of the Ninth of Av I was playing with other children in a lane. Incidentally I have never forgotten the swamps of Pinsk—*Pinsker blotte* was a byword. It was winter. You could not cross the road. We were playing in the narrow lane, in the darkness. And along came the Cossacks at a gallop and jumped right over our heads. So what did I take with me from there? Fear, hunger and fear, fear of Cossacks in Pinsk and of the dreadful cries from the police station.

Of course, I enjoyed the warmth of the family, of Grandfather and uncles and aunts. After all, I was a small child, and life for me was mainly good. But I was deeply conscious of Mother's worries; I was torn between my mother's suffering because of my sister's activities and pride in my sister who was doing something forbidden, but apparently very important. I remember how one of my aunts, who lived in the same house as the Weizmann family, came once and announced that the czar had granted a constitution. That was in 1905; there were great rejoicing in Pinsk and joyful demonstrations, as in all Russia. But it was only a rumor, a trick through which the police subsequently arrested all those who openly wanted a constitution.

I also remember the same aunt coming in one day and sadly

telling us that Herzl was dead. In mourning for Herzl, who died in 1904, my sister wore black until we reached America in 1906. Her costume was the background for the first clash between my sister and father. Father had been in the United States for three years, working in the railroad workshops in Milwaukee. He was a trade union member and already regarded himself as something of an American. Nevertheless, he could not find an apartment for us. So he brought us to his one rented room. This was in July, and a day later he took us to buy American clothes. There was no problem as far as my little sister and I were concerned. But my elder sister, who was a member of a revolutionary movement and had convictions of her own, had arrived in a black dress with long sleeves and a high collar, and Father wanted to change her style. He already felt a little resentful of my sister after Mother's letters, for it was because of her that he had been unable to go back to Russia, and we had come to the United States. I still remember that he chose a straw hat with a broad brim full of all kinds of colored flowers. My sister, of course, refused to wear this creation though Father tried to explain to her that this was America and not Russia, and this was how people had to dress; she would not agree.

A few months later we had another lesson about life in America. In September there was a Labor Day parade with workers' marches. Father told us to stand on a street corner to see him marching legally with his trade union. Our little sister, who had brought the fear of Cossacks with her from Russia, suddenly saw mounted policemen at the head of the procession; she started to scream, "Mommy, the Cossacks are coming!" She developed a fever and was ill for quite a while. Father was very proud of the freedom in America and of the fact that he was an organized worker who could march openly with police present to protect the procession and not to disperse it as in Russia.

By 1906 Father belonged to the synagogue; he had friends, and he was proud of being a free worker, but he could not find an apartment suitable to his means. Finally, Father located vacant rooms behind a store. There was no choice but to take the place; Mother, with her energy and initiative, decided that since a store came with the rooms, she would actually open a shop. So she ran a tiny dairy store. That she did not know a word of English was not important because we lived in a Jewish immigrant quarter, where of course Yiddish was the language spoken. Father objected to the enterprise. "All right," he said, "if you want to open a store, go ahead. I won't have anything to do with it." He went to work, and Mother ran the shop. My sister, who had started studying English in the evenings, was still tied to her movement in Pinsk. She went to work in a sweatshop as a seamstress and sent part of the money she earned to her comrades in Russia.

A little later, five or six years after the 1905 revolution, many members of the Russian revolutionary movement emigrated to America; some also came to Milwaukee. Our house soon became a center for them because of my sister. Most were Jews, but there were also a few Gentile Russians. By then our economic position was fairly good. Father worked, and Mother ran the shop. But the family clashed over my sister's refusal to become a real American. She went on in the same style of life as before, something which Father very much resented. While Mother's main objection was that she might miss the chance of making a good match, her rebellion cut Father deeper. He could not stand the affront she represented: a young girl who stubbornly behaved like an immigrant and absolutely refused to act like other girls of her age. With all his goodness of heart, Father had strict ideas about discipline. He expected obedience from his daughters. The conflict between them became so acute that my sister had to leave home. She did not want to help Mother in the shop; that was against her proletarian ideas. She did not want to dress like an American girl; she did not want to meet any well-to-do, established boy that Mother regarded as a good match. In any case, she was attached to a boy who had remained in Pinsk, who later became her husband. So she left home and went to work in the needle industry.

She was not too competent a garment worker. Every two or three days she would stick her finger under the needle of the machine and puncture her finger instead of the cloth—which led to infections and all kinds of trouble. She would come home for a while and then leave again. I was the go-between, and every now and then I would try to soften Father, who loved all his children very much, though they did not always get on together. Even when I was a little girl, I had some influence on my father. I would often sit on his knee and try to persuade him to ask my sister to come home, for she would never agree to come home when she was in difficulties unless Father invited her. More than once I managed to induce Father to send a note to tell her to come home.

I did these things because I loved my sister; besides, we had a common front. I hated Mother's shop like poison. Since Father refused to have anything to do with it, he would leave for work early in the morning while Mother had to go to market to buy groceries for the shop. I would be left alone in the morning to look after the customers, which I resented. Because of the shop I was often late for school—a terrible disgrace. I was ashamed to be late. Mother did not take the matter seriously; she used to say, *"Vestu vern a rebbetzin mit a tog shpeter"*—"So it'll take you one more day to become a learned dame." In other words: "What's the difference?" Nevertheless, I managed to get good marks. Somehow I made it. But the shame of coming to class late, not once or twice, but sometimes more than twice a week hurt me bitterly. So I had common ground with my sister; she didn't want to be in the shop, and I hated the shop. It was a kind of class struggle for the right to be a proletarian and not a petty shopkeeper. In addition, my sister's plight troubled me because I saw the harsh conditions in which she lived. She was not very strong physically. Finally she had to go to the tuberculosis sanitarium in Denver. When she recovered, she married the boy from Pinsk, who had joined her in Colorado.

Later there were clashes between my parents and me. When I finished elementary school, I wanted to go to high school. Almost from the first day I registered in primary school I made up my mind to be a teacher. In those years there was a law in the state of Wisconsin that a married woman could not be a teacher. Mother was terribly worried: if I became a teacher, that meant I would not get married. When I graduated from elementary school, Mother decided that I should not go to high school, because if I did, there was a real danger that I might succeed in becoming a teacher and a spinster; instead, I was to go to commercial school to learn secretarial work and become a stenographer or a typist. For me this prospect was worse than death.

Father agreed that there was no future in my becoming a teacher; anyway, he supported Mother. Then we had a really big quarrel. I tried to become as independent as possible financially. I would work after school, on school holidays, and during the summer vacation so as not to take spending money from my parents.

Finally, I reached a point when I couldn't get on with my parents any longer. My sister in Denver had a family by this time, but I had corresponded clandestinely with her from the time she left Milwaukee, though she had broken with our parents. I was about twelve when she left. I wrote to my sister secretly from a friend's address. In those days, of course, I did not even have money for stamps; my mother still had the shop, and I confess today—it is a good thing there is a statute of limitations—that I would regularly take two or three cents from the till to buy stamps. Nor was this all my crime. Before her marriage my sister's situation was very difficult. She had no work, and she was sick. So I would buy a few extra stamps to put in the envelope. My sister had always been very strict in her notions of morality. In a letter she wrote me, she hoped I was doing nothing wrong to procure money for the stamps. I doubled my offense by lying to her and writing that I was sinless. But there was no other way of maintaining contact with her; I had no source of livelihood, and neither had she. After her marriage, when my parents opposed my wish to go to high school, we cooked up a plan according to which I would run away to her in Denver, where I would be able to continue high school while living with her.

My flight was no simple matter. When I decided to take this

step, Shaina sent me a railway ticket. I could not tell my parents that I was going off to my sister—I would never have managed it. There was nothing to do but to run away from home. At that time we lived above the shop—the bedrooms were on the second floor. I arranged with a girlfriend to lower my bundle of clothes to her through the window in the evening; we would take it to the railway station, and in the morning, instead of going to school, I would go to the station. That evening I sat in the kitchen, in the presence of my father and mother, writing a letter telling them that I was going away to Shaina and that they should not worry about me. In the morning, instead of going to school, I went, as planned, to the railway station. I had no experience of timetables, and I was still sitting in the station at the time when the letter reached my parents. Fortunately for me, they did not come to look for me until the school inquired as to my absence, but by then I was gone.

My act was a great blow to my parents and to my little sister, who remained alone in the house. On the other hand, her life became easier as a result. Father was not so strict with her, and Mother too treated her more indulgently than her two elder daughters. I was away from home for about a year and a half; Father absolutely refused to write to me. I corresponded with Mother, but Father would not write a word. I was not surprised because Father was very proud; he was deeply hurt not only because of his love for me, but because of my behavior: How could a girl act this way? One day I got a letter from Father telling me that if I cared for Mother's life, I must come back home at once. I understood that if Father was actually writing to me, the situation must be critical, so I returned home. From that time on I no longer had to fight for my freedom or the right to do what I wanted.

When I came back from Denver, I went back to high school without any opposition from Father and Mother. They saw that they could not prevent this step. After graduation, I continued in the Teachers' Training College that was part of the university in Madison. I had many friends, boys and girls, and I got along well with the Gentile students. Personally, I experienced no anti-Semitism in the college. I don't remember a single instance when students or teachers made an offensive remark. Nevertheless, perhaps because of the atmosphere at home, and because I was deeply involved in movement activities from an early age, life outside school had a much greater influence on me than life in the school itself. I went to college to get a professional education—that was all.

Ours was a traditional Jewish home. The language in the house was Yiddish, although we had received an English education. My father had sent my little sister and me to a Talmud Torah because there was no other Hebrew school. I cannot boast of having learned a great deal of Hebrew at that Talmud Torah, but we learned Yiddish at home. We read a Yiddish newspaper every day, and we had Yiddish books—in short, the whole house was run in that language.

In those days, when a Socialist-Zionist speaker came to town, he would not go to a hotel. He stayed at private homes. We had a famous couch, and the Lord knows who did not sleep on it. The house was full of life, for we were never a family that restricted itself to its own private affairs. Both Father and Mother were socially active. Mother's hands were always busy; she would be helping in a bazaar or an affair for some worthy enterprise. And she was an excellent housewife, famous for her fish, which she usually cooked on Fridays for the Sabbath meal.

Father and Mother were very well thought of in the city. For instance, we had a rabbi, the late Rabbi Schonfeld, who was a wonderful man, as well as a great scholar. When Syrkin or Zhitlovski* would come to Milwaukee, they would visit him. He was very strict in religious matters, would not drink anything outside his own home, and hardly ever went out to give sermons at weddings. To Mother's great joy—she used to talk about it till her dying day—Rabbi Schonfeld came to our home for my wedding, drank a little, and, even more, offered to make a speech. That was a great event. My parents were respected in the community; they had an open house, open hearts, and open

---

* Nachman Syrkin (1868–1924), ideological founder of Socialist Zionism. Chaim Zhitlovski (1865–1943), a foremost exponent of Diaspora nationalism.

hands. Both had a wonderful sense of humor. Mother had a ringing laugh, and there was always a song on her lips. Most important, I cannot remember any period when we thought only of our personal affairs. Our home was always involved in causes of some kind.

After I came back to Milwaukee from Denver, my relations with my father became harmonious. We cooperated in public activities during World War I. At that time the Joint Distribution Committee was the major organization for helping European Jews; it was totally different then from what it became in World War II or later. In those days the Joint was a very bureaucratic organization, subject to a great deal of vigorous criticism because of its high-handed methods. A more popular new organization called the People's Relief was set up, mainly by Jewish workers. In Milwaukee we joined the popular body, which was run by a committee of representatives of various organizations in the city. Father was a representative of his trade union, and though I was still a teen-ager, I too belonged, not as a member of a political party but merely as a member of a literary society which held lectures and debates of a nonpolitical nature. My father and I worked together in the People's Relief all through the war, and I was very happy at this collaboration. We had no arguments over principles. I devoted much of my time after school to this organization by helping in the office.

In those days the movement for a World Jewish Congress also started. Rutenberg* was one of its chief proponents, so was Shmaria Levin. In American Jewish public life the idea of a World Jewish Congress was opposed by the well-established Jews of German origin—the group whose members became the leaders of the American Jewish Committee. Jewish Socialist workers, who then were ideologically anti-Zionist, were not against a Jewish Congress, but they opposed a pro-Palestine plank in its platform. There was much agitation among American Jews around this issue in those years, with popular elections of representatives to the Congress held for the first time in 1918.

* Pinhas Rutenberg (1879–1942). A leading figure in the Jewish community of Palestine who founded the Palestine Electric Company.

In Milwaukee we ran a single list composed of all the various Zionist groups and Jewish organizations that were not opposed to Zionism against the list of the anti-Zionist Jewish Socialists.

Though Father was active in the Congress movement and we worked together in complete harmony, he had his own notions of fitting behavior for young girls. At that time it was quite common to make speeches on street corners because then you didn't have to hire a hall. On one evening when I was about to leave the house, he asked me where I was going. I told him that I had to speak at a street-corner meeting. (We would set up a table or a cart with a table on it and begin to speak as soon as a few people collected. After a while an audience would gather, as in Hyde Park in London.) When Father heard of my intention, he stormed: "What? *Mabovitch's tochter?* [Mabovitch's daughter?] Stand in the street?" I tried to explain. "You shan't go," he insisted. I said, "Father, I will go." And poor Mother stood between Father and me, two stubborn people. Father threatened to pull me down by my braid if I dared to appear. I believed him because he generally kept his promises, good or bad. I warned my comrades who were waiting on the street corner that there would probably be a scandal. Someone else opened the meeting, and I was the second or third speaker. I got up and made my speech—I was terribly nervous—but nothing happened. When I came home, it was pretty late. Mother was waiting up for me. Father was asleep. She told me that he came home and said, *"Ich vais nit fun vanit nemt sich dos zu ihr"*—"I don't know where she gets it from." That meant I had been so successful in convincing my father by this speech of mine that he forgot to pull me off the platform. I always say that this was the most successful speech of my life.

Our house continued to be a center for friends although the intellectual climate changed somewhat. In the early years, when my sister was still at home, the visitors used to be Russian immigrants who were social revolutionaries. Later, when my sister went to Denver, it became a center for members of the Labor-Zionist Poale Zion and the Territorialists—who had been willing to accept Uganda instead of Palestine as the Jewish homeland—even before I joined the Poale Zion. Though for a long time I could not make up my mind to enroll formally in the party, the house was a gathering place for the movement. We would go out with comrades on Sundays for a picnic; Father and Mother always went along and joined in the singing and gaiety.

Father did not object when I finally joined the Poale Zion. I had refused to join the party until I had firmly decided to go to Palestine. My ideas of Zionism at that time were quite primitive. I did not understand how one could be a Zionist and not go to settle in Palestine. I had no taste for parlor Zionism. In 1917 Ben Zvi and Ben-Gurion came to Milwaukee to seek disciples. Milwaukee was a good Zionist city, and the Socialist Poale Zion had a solid branch whose members responded to the Palestinians. When I joined the party, I knew that I would go to Palestine at the first opportunity after World War I. This decision saddened my parents greatly, especially because Shaina decided at the same time that she too would go with her two children, a boy aged two and a girl of ten. My youngest sister was studying at the university in Madison. We planned that as soon as she finished her studies, she would join us as well. My parents saw their home and their family collapsing, but they did not protest.

Father was no weakling. He had a strong character and was able to bear pain. But when Father accompanied my husband and me to the railroad station, he didn't say a word. He just stood and wept. Of course, I had expected Mother to cry, but Father wept too. We arrived in Palestine in '21 and our parents in '26.

So I left the United States fully conscious of the meaning of America, its freedom, its opportunities, the beauty of its countryside. I loved America, but—perhaps it is not tactful to say this—although we have been here for forty-five years, neither my sister nor I have ever known a single moment of homesickness, not a moment—not because we belittle what America gave us, but from the day we came to Palestine it was so natural to be here. This was how it had to be.

We left New York on the nineteenth of May, 1921, just after the May Day riots in Palestine. Everybody thought we were more or less crazy. Who sailed at such a risky time?

We had an eventful journey to Palestine on the SS *Pocahontas*, a ship thoroughly unseaworthy as its many mishaps and accidents testified. It took us a week to sail from New York to Boston; at this point several would-be pioneers in our group lost heart and got off instead of continuing on our dangerous course. My sister with the children was urged to get off at Boston, for it was obvious that the ship was in bad shape. But, as I said, she inherited a large measure of Father's obstinacy, and she refused to disembark. It proved to be a perilous journey full of peculiar adventures. My brother-in-law remained in America, for in 1921 it was impossible for a family with two children to just pack up and go. He had to stay in the United States for a time to help support the family with his earnings.

I shall never forget the moment when we arrived at the luxurious Tel Aviv railway station on the fourteenth of July, nearly two months after we had set out. Sand, blazing sand—that was all. One comrade who was part of our group turned to me and said: "Well, Golda, you wanted to come to *Eretz Yisroel*. Here we are. Now we can go back—it's enough." But he stayed all his life, and he died here, in Palestine.

Even before we left America, my husband and I had decided to go to a kibbutz. At that time no one knew clearly what a kibbutz was. We arrived in July, and in those days new members were not accepted by a kibbutz in the middle of the year; at Rosh Hashanah the kibbutz would know who was leaving and could tell how much room there would be for new members. We applied to Merhavia. Three general meetings of the kibbutz members were held to determine whether to accept us or not, not because there was anything against Myerson, but I was an American girl and the kibbutzniks doubted whether an American girl would seriously want to work hard and fit into their life. Finally, at the third meeting, they decided to accept us. I think what settled the matter in our favor was the phonograph we brought with us. It was the first phonograph without a horn in the country, and we had many good records. The phonograph is still in Merhavia.

Before we joined Merhavia, all of us—my sister with her two children, a family of friends, Myerson and I—stayed in Tel Aviv. Apartments in Tel Aviv at that time cost five pounds sterling a month, with a year's rent payable in advance. True, we had come from America, but we had brought no millions with us. Finally, we got a couple of rooms in Neveh Tzedek, in Lilienblum Street. The kitchen and conveniences were located outside in the yard. There we settled down. Thanks to the phonograph, the house was full every evening with all the Jews of Tel Aviv—that's how it seemed to me—who used to come to listen to our records. Many years later I would still meet people I did not recognize, who would tell me: "But we listened to records in your home."

If my conscience hurt me for giving pain to Father and Mother when we sailed away, it hurt me again to leave my sister, with her two small children, one only two years old, when we joined Merhavia. She went to work at the Hadassah Hospital; her boy developed a local eye disease. But I would not give up my plan to go to the kibbutz, for Eretz Israel and the kibbutz were a single ideal for me. So we went to Merhavia.

To be honest, we endured no real hardship; we lived the way all other members of the kibbutz lived—not a life of ease, but one we had chosen. However, my sister and her children had a very bad time, and it needed a great deal of courage for her to stay on and not go back to America. My brother-in-law was still working in the United States, where they had managed to live modestly but decently. But she never once thought of giving up; she kept going with two small children, of whom one had eye trouble and the other suffered all the time from boils—also a local infection; she stayed in the town fighting her war for existence, until my brother-in-law came. She was a real heroine.

We did not tell our parents about our troubles; I remember

how when I was in Merhavia I once wrote home about our way of life in the kibbutz. My mother really got a shock: that I should be doing the washing for everybody and baking all the bread! At that time the kibbutz had only thirty-two members.

Many years later this business of baking bread caused a sensation in a quite different place. That was in Moscow in 1948, when I came there as minister after the establishment of the state with my daughter, who was a member of the Negev kibbutz of Revivim. Once, at a reception, the Russian women started asking her what she did at her kibbutz. They thought that because she was the daughter of a minister, she must be something like the chairman of a kolkhoz. I explained that, on the contrary, she worked in the fields and baked bread. It so happened that she had worked in the bakery. They were as shocked as my mother who could not understand why I should be baking the bread, doing the washing and other physical work.

Our parents joined us several years later. Their motives were partly Zionist and partly personal—they wanted to be with us. If we had remained in the United States, they would probably not have packed up and left. The Zion Commonwealth Society sold plots of land in America, and Father bought two plots of ten dunams in Herzliya, which was nothing but sand at the time, and another plot in Afula, hardly more than a dusty spot. On the plan, Father's house in Afula was supposed to be exactly opposite a projected opera house, which was never built. Since I knew what kind of a "city" Afula was, I had a pretty good notion of the likelihood of an opera house in Afula.

To my regret, I had to leave the kibbutz for personal reasons. When our parents came, we were living in Jerusalem, and my sister was in Tel Aviv with her family. Together we persuaded Father to forget about the opera house and to build a house in Herzliya. Father's house, which he mostly built himself, was one of the first three or four houses in District Gimel of Herzliya. Since he owned an area of ten dunams, he also had an orange grove; both he and Mother immediately became two of the most active of the first settlers there. As there was no *hazan* in the synagogue, Father became the synagogue cantor. When we came to visit them, the grandchildren delighted in Grandfather, who sang so beautifully, and his house again became a real family center.

At festivals, Passover, and Rosh Hashanah, our two families would come with our children to Father's house in Herzliya. To this day, both my sister's children and my own son and daughter have the dearest memories of Father's house—memories of festivals, with Grandmother's fish and Grandmother's strudel—and they can still hum Father's tunes. At the Seder, when we read the Hagadah, and on Friday nights, they still remember those days.

Security was not too good in Herzliya because it lay between two Arab villages, and it was pretty hard to pass through them. Father worked, and after a while, to help make ends meet, Mother used to serve meals. Since Father's house was on a hill, the Haganah put their "slick" (the hiding place for weapons) in his house. Till close to his dying day, Father never missed his turn of guard duty at night. During the disturbances of '29 the women and children were evacuated from his section of Herzliya, but Mother refused to go and stayed in the house with Father.

By that time I was working in the Histadrut. Father was pleased at this; he too was a Histadrut member, for he belonged to a cooperative of carpenters, so he took my work as a matter of course. Mother was not always happy about my activities, especially after the children were born, because I was not much at home, but Father understood. He even took pride in me.

A few years later, I appeared as a witness during the British trial of Richlin and Sirkin, two young Palestinians accused of stealing arms for the Haganah. The next day I came to Herzliya and saw Father; he said nothing to me. But Mother told me later that from early that morning, as soon as *Davar* arrived, he kept showing the newspaper to the neighbors: "Look, my Golda!"

Father was well aware of what was going on in the country,

and though he may have thought my work dangerous, he understood our position. He knew what the Haganah and the Histadrut meant.

Father died at the age of seventy-nine, and until the last six months of his life when he fell ill, he was strong, upright, handsome. During a demonstration in Migdiel Father marched a long distance in protest against the British and was always active in the struggle for Jewish labor. Throughout the years he lived in this country he conscientiously performed all the good deeds demanded of Jews in the homeland.

Father died before the establishment of the state of Israel. I have always viewed my membership in the government as a job that had to be done, but I have often thought of what it would have meant to Father if he had lived to see the creation of a Jewish state, with a Jewish government, and with his daughter a member of that government.

To what extent did Father and Mother make me what I am? I would not like to put all the responsibility on them, but perhaps one of the fundamental principles I learned from home was not to shut myself up within the limits of personal matters or family affairs. My movement background came more from my sister than from my parents. From my father I got, let us say, my obstinacy. Insofar as I have shown the quality of firmness, it came mainly from him. From Mother I got my optimism. There was never a sign of depression in the house, even in the hardest times. In any case, it is perfectly clear to me that all the positive features, insofar as they exist, came from my family, my parents and my sisters. If I have added anything negative, that is not their fault. They had no hand in it.

I am not sure that Mother was always pleased with me. Often, before we came to this country and afterward as well, when she would see me working hard and sometimes, as she thought, neglecting my home and my children, she would ask me: "*Goldah'le, vos vet zein die tachlis fun dir?*" ("What will be the end of you?") I am not sure if the end would have satisfied her. But I have taken something, I think, from all the members of my family: Father and Mother, my sisters, my brother-in-law, and my husband, who was not a public figure but a retiring individual, with a deep appreciation of art, music, and literature. I met my husband when I was very young, only fifteen. I was always grateful to him for giving me much that I did not get from my home. I can say that I was fortunate in the sense that I was able to get so much from the people around me, both friends and family.

I returned to Poland for the first time at the beginning of 1939 when I was on a speaking tour for the party; Pinsk was of course included in my route. I set out on my tour, but only reached Lodz, for I fell ill on the way and spent two weeks in bed in Lodz. In the meantime, my visa expired and the Poles refused to renew it, so I never got to Pinsk. In 1948, when I went to Moscow as the Israeli minister, it was no simple matter to move freely in Russia. I hoped that in time I would have a chance to see my hometown again. But my service in Moscow was suddenly cut short. I had come to Moscow in the beginning of September; in January, after the elections in Israel, Ben-Gurion summoned me home to join the government as Minister of Labor. All I could do was to wind up my affairs in Moscow. Yet even if I had visited Pinsk at that time, I would have found no one of my family left in Pinsk, except perhaps one man, the grandson of my grandmother's sister. All the rest were killed in the Holocaust. Nevertheless, I very much wanted to go back at least once.

2. How I Made It in My Kibbutz

Memories of Merhavia related by Mrs. Meir at a holiday meeting in the kibbutz of Revivim. (In Hebrew, 1971)

Fifty years ago I lived long enough in Merhavia to be able to say that I was really there. In those days it was a kvutzah.* Today there are a kibbutz and a moshav† of that name.

Our present celebration is really a festival of all Israel. Without the immense will of the men and women of the labor settlements, it is doubtful whether the Histadrut could have arisen and attained the position it holds at present. Today values have changed. If we went out on Dizengoff Street in Tel Aviv or any street in Jerusalem or Haifa and took a public opinion poll on the importance of the kibbutz or the moshav, I am no longer sure as to the reply.

When, while still in America, I decided to settle in Palestine, I knew that I would go to a cooperative settlement. I chose Merhavia because a friend from Milwaukee was already there. To my astonishment, Myerson and I were not immediately accepted. As we had arrived in July, we were told that no applications could be considered in the middle of summer. We

---

* Kvutzah is a collective agricultural settlement; the term is used interchangeably with kibbutz.

† Moshav is an agricultural settlement which combines private ownership with cooperative farming.

would have to wait till Rosh Hashanah, when the kvutzah knew who was staying and who was going, so that new members could be accepted in place of those who were leaving. Meanwhile, we went to Tel Aviv, then being built. Our group from the United States made a tremendous impression in the Tel Aviv of the time. One day I met a Tel Aviv woman who, upon learning that I had come from the United States, clapped her hands in astonishment: "Thank God, now the redemption is near—at last Jews have come from America (the millionaires). Now it will be all right."

I gave private English lessons in those days, after rejecting an offer to teach in Herzliya High School. Though I had to work to make a living, I did not want to become a full-time teacher. Shortly before Rosh Hashanah, we applied to Merhavia to be accepted as members and again received a negative reply. Only two members supported us; one of them was my friend. One reason for the rejection was that this community of unmarried men and women did not at that time want families. Babies were a luxury the young kibbutz could not afford. The greatest opposition came from the "veteran" women, who had been in the country all of eight years; they could not imagine that an American girl would do the hard physical work required.

Despite the rejection, we were invited to come to Merhavia for two or three days so that the members could look us over. I well remember my first day's work. It was the threshing season, and they told me to "sit" on the board of the threshing machine that revolved in the barn and threshed the grain. My efforts at work did not make as great an impression on the young men as the phonograph and records we brought with us. It was the first time anyone had arrived with a hornless phonograph, which aroused general admiration. Of course, they would have been happy to accept the phonograph as a dowry without the bride who owned it, but we wouldn't agree to that. They finally accepted us after a third meeting of the whole kvutzah. After that I had to be careful not to make any slip expected of an American girl.

I forced myself to eat every kind of food or dish, even if it was hard to look at, let alone swallow. The food generally had a most unpleasant taste because of the oil we bought from the Arabs: It was not refined, kept in leather bags and bitter as gall, but it was the base for all our dishes.

Every month a different member took her turn in the kitchen. Conditions there were so grueling that two weeks before her turn came round the girl in question would generally become depressed. With plain common sense I decided to take things as they came, including kitchen duty. I never considered work in the kitchen demeaning.

There were few possibilities in the kitchen; the main raw ingredients for cooking were: sour cereals, bitter oil, a few vegetables from our small vegetable patch, tinned bully beef from British Army surpluses, and canned herring mysteriously called "fresh" which was herring in tomato sauce. First, I scratched the oil from the menu so the bitter taste disappeared. Then I declared war on the "fresh" for breakfast—a nightmare in the cold, damp winter days. Instead, I bought Quaker Oats and cooked hot porridge in the morning. The novelty aroused opposition, which soon gave place, however, to approval of the "children's pap." One dish that was regularly served was quinine because of the malaria we all contracted owing to the swampy land.

In those days we drank from enamel mugs, which looked fine and shiny so long as they were new, but after a little while began to chip and rust and became repulsive. I decided to stop buying these mugs; although we sometimes reached a state when we were left with two or three glasses, from which we drank in turn, for the whole kvutzah I bought nothing but glasses.

Another "bourgeois" feature I introduced into our kvutzah was a white sheet spread as a tablecloth on Friday night, with a vase of wild flowers—that adornment gave us a bad name throughout the Emek.* I also insisted on ironing my dress or blouse carefully. This was also viewed as a "bourgeois" weakness.

---

* The Jezreel Valley, site of many kibbutzim.

The farm was not particularly well developed, and we lived mainly on work for the Jewish National Fund, digging holes for planting trees. The holes naturally had to be dug in a rocky hill and be dug deep enough to hold their shape. After a day's work of this kind I used to long to wash and have a rest, but I overcame such desires and went to help in the kitchen, though I was so tired that an ordinary fork seemed to weigh a ton. But you get used even to such hard work.

In the course of time I went on to work in the poultry yard. Before I came here, I could never bear to stay in the same room with a living bird (or a living mouse). Nevertheless, I went to study poultry breeding in Ben Shemen. During the course we did practical work in the hen run. At Merhavia we had the first incubator in the Emek; it could hatch five hundred eggs. People came to our poultry house from all the villages, and I don't know what attracted them more: the chicks we sold or our phonograph records.

We had an American poultry expert at Merhavia, who wanted to become a member. Morning, noon, and night he would lecture us, especially at meals in the dining hall, and talk to us about the importance of protein for the chickens. Finally, a girl got up from the table in anger and exclaimed: "I can't sit with you when you use such coarse language."

There was an interim period when Myerson and I were in Tel Aviv; there I bore my son, Menahem. When he was four months old, I took him back to Merhavia. The children lived in one room and I in the room next door, so that I could keep an eye on them night and day. Under the hygienic conditions of those days, I used to bathe the children in a tin bath. After each child's bath I would pour alcohol into the bath to disinfect it. Since alcohol was an expensive commodity and I used it in no small quantities, there was a rumor in the kvutzah that "Golda gives the children alcohol to drink."

I remember some of the members of the kvutzah. There was one fellow from Brooklyn who was very talented, but not good at harnessing mules. He had to take the milk in a cart to the train early in the morning, so that it should get to Haifa the same day. One day, when he reached the wooden bridge over the wadi, the mules refused to budge, and while he was trying to persuade them, they broke free from the harness and went back to the stable, leaving him with all his gear beside the bridge. Another member in a moment of rage against his mule burst out: "Either you or I—the two of us can't stay in Merhavia."

The two members who stood guard at night were given two eggs for their supper. This was a great luxury, and there were always people ready to share that nocturnal omelet. I was always willing to come to the kitchen even at one o'clock in the morning to chat and eat with the guards. And the guards liked me, at least during their time on guard duty. Of course, I was warned against wearing a white dress at night because that made too good a target for Arab snipers.

3. Women's Lib—1930

This article originally appeared in English in The Ploughwoman, *a collection of personal narratives by women pioneers in Palestine. (Published by the Pioneer Women's Organization)*

Taken as a whole, the inner struggles and despairs of a mother who goes to work have few parallels. But within that whole there are many shades and variations. There are some mothers who work only when they are forced to, when the husband is sick or unemployed or else when the family has in some other way gone off the track of a normal life. In such cases the mother feels her course of action justified by necessity—her children would not be fed otherwise. But there is a type of woman who cannot remain at home for other reasons. In spite of the place which her children and her family take up in her life, her nature and being demand something more; she cannot divorce herself from a larger social life. She cannot let her children narrow her horizon. And for such a woman, there is no rest.

Theoretically it looks straightforward enough. The woman who replaces her with the children is devoted, loves the children, is reliable and suited to the work; the children are fully looked after. And there are even pedagogic theorists who claim that it is actually better for the children not to have their mother constantly hovering over them. And a mother who is occupied outside the house of course has the great advantage of being able to develop. In any case, the constant danger of retrogression is lessened; therefore, she can bring more to her children than if she were to remain at home. Everything seems all right. But one look of reproach from the little one when the mother goes away and leaves it with a stranger is enough to throw down the whole structure of vindication. That look, that plea to the mother to stay, can be withstood only by an almost superhuman effort of will.

I am not speaking now of the constant worry that something may have happened to her child in her absence. And I need not bring in her feelings when her child falls sick—the flood of self-reproach and self-accusation. At the best of times, in the best circumstances, there is a perpetual consciousness at the back of her mind that her child lacks a mother's tenderness. We believe, above all, in education by example, therefore we must ask ourselves: Whose example molds the child of the working mother? A "borrowed" mother becomes the model. The cute things a child says reach the mother at second hand. Such a child does not know the magic healing power of a mother's kiss, which takes away the pain of a bruise. And there are times, after a wearying, care-filled day, when the mother looks at her child almost as if she did not recognize it; a feeling of alienation from her nearest and dearest steals into her heart.

And having admitted all this, we ask: Can the mother of today remain at home all day with her children? Can she compel herself to be other than she is because she has become a mother? That feeling of alienation between mother and child can occur, and often does occur in an even more serious form, when the mother always stays at home and cannot develop with her children. Inevitably the modern woman asks herself: Is there something wrong with me if my children don't fill up my life? Am I at fault, if after giving them, and the one other person nearest to me a place in my heart, some part of me still demands to be filled by activities outside the family and the home? Can we today measure our devotion to husband and children by our indifference to everything else? Is it not often true that a woman who has given up all the outside world for her husband and her children has done so not out of a sense of duty, out of devotion and love, but out of incapacity, because her soul is not able to take into itself the many-sidedness of life, with its sufferings and with its joys? If a woman does remain exclusively with her children and gives herself to nothing else, does that really prove that she is more devoted than the conventional mother? And if a wife has no intimate friends, does that prove that she has a greater love for her husband?

Yet a working mother suffers even in her chosen activity. She always has the feeling that her work is not as productive as that of a man or even of an unmarried woman. And she always responds to her children's natural demands, in health and even more in sickness. This eternal inner division, this double pull, this alternating feeling of unfilled duty—today toward her family, the next day toward her work—this is the burden of the working mother.

4. "A Nice, Law-Abiding Lady"

A part of the testimony given by Mrs. Meir at the Sirkin-Richlin arms trial during which two young Palestinian Jews were accused of stealing arms from the British Army in order to turn them over to the Haganah. (In English, September, 1943)

At the Sirkin-Richlin arms trial (September, 1943) during which two young Palestinians were accused of stealing arms from the British Army in order to turn them over to the Haganah, the prosecutor did not hesitate to suggest that one of the reasons for Jewish volunteering was the desire to obtain arms.

The trial provided one of the first large-scale public opportunities to see Mrs. Meir in one of her most effective aspects—that of facing the government with courage and candor and yet remaining intellectually in command of the situation so as to prevent any blundering admission. A part of the testimony reads:

Q: You are a nice, peaceful, law-abiding lady, are you not?
A: I think I am.
Q: And you have always been so?
A: I have never been accused of anything.
Major Baxter: Well, listen to this from a speech of yours on May 2, 1940 (reading out of a file): "We, the workers, will combat any appearances of Fascism. The whole Yishuv

46

will join hands in fighting the White Paper. If the Revisionists interfere, we will fight them too. For twenty years we were led to trust the British government, but we have been betrayed. The Ben Shemen case is an example of this." Ben Shemen is where much arms were found, isn't it?

A: I do not know how many arms were found in Ben Shemen.

Q: Now listen to what you said on May 2, 1940: "We never taught our youth the use of firearms for offense but for defensive purpose only."

A: That is right.

Q: "And if they are criminals, then all the Jews in Palestine are criminals." What about that?

A: If a Jew who is armed in self-defense is a criminal, then all the Jews in Palestine are criminals.

Q: Were you yourself trained in the use of arms?

A: I do not know whether I am required to answer to that question. In any case I have never used firearms.

Q: Have you trained the Jewish youth in the use of firearms?

A: Jewish youth will defend Jewish life and property in the event of riots and the necessity to defend life and property. I, as well as other Jews, would defend myself.

President of the Court: Please reply only to the questions.

Q: Do you remember what quantity of firearms was found in Ben Shemen?

A: I don't know.

Q: And if you had been asked in the middle of your speech how much arms were found in Ben Shemen, what would you have replied?

A: What I answered you.

Major Baxter (reading again from the CID file): "Macdonald and his friends are mistaken if they think they can do as they like with us. There are not enough prisons and concentration camps in Palestine to hold all the Jews who are ready to defend their lives and property." Right?

A: If a Jew or Jewess who uses firearms to defend himself against firearms is a criminal, then many new prisons will be needed.

Q: Do you mean to say that there are many firearms?

A: There are many who are ready to defend themselves.

Q: Is the accused, Sirkin, known to you?

A: He is known to me. He is a member of the Histadrut.

Major Baxter (continuing to read from the CID file): "We must do all in our power to help the illegal immigrants. Britain is trying to prevent the growth and expansion of the Jewish community in Palestine, but it should remember that Jews were here two thousand years before the British came."

Showing Mrs. Myerson a photograph of Tennenbaum, Major Baxter asked her:

Do you know this man? Have you ever heard his name?

A: I do not know him. I read the name in the papers—never before.

Q: Do you have an intelligence service in the Histadrut?

A: No.

Q: What?

A: You heard: No!

Q: Have you heard of "Haganah"?

A: Yes.

Q: Do they have arms?

A: I don't know, but I suppose they have.

Q: Have you heard of "Palmach"?

A: Yes.

Q: What is it?

A: I first heard of the Palmach as groups of young people, organized with the knowledge of the authorities, and who were specially trained at the time the German Army was drawing near to Palestine. Its function was to help the British Army in any way necessary should the evil happen and the enemy invade the country.

Q: And are these groups still in existence?

A: I do not know.

Q: Is this a legal organization?

A: All I know is that these groups were organized to help the British Army and with the knowledge of the authorities.

Q: Can members of the Histadrut be members of "Haganah" or "Palmach"?

A: Yes, it may be that there are members of the Histadrut who are also members of Haganah and Palmach.

Q: And they are ready to do all that you said in your speech, which I read before?

A: They are prepared to defend themselves when attacked. We have had very bad experiences in this country. I came to Palestine in 1921, shortly after riots and bloodshed. The Jewish community in Palestine has been attacked many times. There were also disturbances which continued for years. When I say we are ready to defend, I want to make myself clear. This defense is not merely theoretical. We still remember the riots of 1921, 1922, and 1929 and the four years of disturbances from 1936 to 1939. Everybody in Palestine knows, as do the authorities, that not only would there have been nothing left, but Jewish honor would have been blemished had there not been people ready for defense, and if brave Jewish youths had not defended the Jewish settlements.

Q: Don't you know that government has provided 30,000 Jewish armed special constables?

A: Yes, I know, and I also know that before 1936 government was also providing for us. But no one in government can deny the fact that if the Jews had not been prepared to defend themselves, terrible things would have happened to us. Furthermore, we are very proud of the Jews of the Warsaw Ghetto who stood up against their persecutors, practically unarmed, and we are certain that they took example from the Jewish self-defense in Palestine.

Q: Do you also have respect for the Jews who have stolen 300 rifles and ammunition from the Army?

A: Certainly not; stealing from the Army is a crime in our eyes.

Q: But these arms might be useful for the Haganah?

A: This should not be done. There is not a Jew who is not interested in this war and in the victory of the British forces.

Q: You wouldn't say, would you, that the rifles walked off by themselves?

Major Baxter: (showing the witness Sirkin's exemption card): This exemption card seems to indicate that you had conscription?

A: It is no secret that the Jewish Agency had for some time been conducting a campaign for enlistment and that every able-bodied Jew was ordered to place himself in the armed force.

Q: And anyone who didn't have an exemption card was beaten up?

A: The Jewish Agency, the Histadrut, and all other responsible bodies more than once condemned publicly the acts of violence which had occurred. We were interested in educating public opinion towards joining up.

President of the Court: Don't you think that the government is the best judge of whether there should be conscription or not? Would it not have been wiser to follow loyally the government decision not to have conscription in this country?

A: We are not in a position to impose conscription in Palestine, but on the other hand both the government and the Army asked for Jews to go into the forces and asked the Agency to help, and we thought it right to tell the Jews that this was their war.

Q: Do you call it volunteering when a man is dismissed from his job on account of his refusal to enlist?

A: We considered such dismissals as moral pressure, since always and among every people there are young men who find it more convenient to stay home, to shirk their duty and spend their time in the streets and cafés. We have been at war with Hitler since 1933, without any declaration of war and without the possibility of fighting back.

Reexamined by the defense counsel, Dr. Joseph, Mrs. Myerson said that even high British Army officers had taken part in the Jewish Agency recruiting campaign and that some of them had come to the Histadrut to ask for its advice and help in recruiting Jews to the British Army. She also said that there was a Jewish representative at Sarafand on behalf of the Jewish Agency.

Dr. Joseph: Is it true that there was a terrible massacre and almost all the Jewish population killed in Hebron only because there was no Jewish self-defense there?

A: Yes, that was in 1929, and the same thing happened the same year in Safad; in 1936 there was a night of terrible slaughter in the Jewish quarter of Tiberias, and all this could only happen because there was no Haganah in those places.

Q: Did Haganah also have arms before the outbreak of war?

A: I do not know, but I suppose that it did. There were also riots before the war.

President of the Court: Can we not limit ourselves only to what concerns this case?

Dr. Joseph: It was not I but the prosecutor who brought up the political question.

President: I ask you to limit yourself only to what concerns this case and not to go backwards, or otherwise we'll soon be back to a period of two thousand years ago.

G.M.: If the Jewish question had been solved two thousand years ago . . .

President: Keep quiet!

G.M.: I object to being addressed in that manner.

President: You should know how to conduct yourself in court.

G.M.: I beg your pardon if I interrupted you, but you should not address me in that manner.

5. The Goal of Jewish Workers

As the Jewish struggle against the mandatory government developed, the Anglo-American Committee of Inquiry held hearings in Jerusalem. Mrs. Meir spoke to the commission as the representative of the Histadrut. (In English, March 25, 1946)

The Palestine Post *described the effect of her testimony:*

"With her direct approach to the essence of the Jewish problem, her assumption that it was understandable and human, and in her clear and unevasive replies, Mrs. Golda Myerson, the only woman to testify before the Inquiry Committee in Jerusalem yesterday morning, dispelled the uncomfortable court-room atmosphere, the irritation and the boredom that had latterly prevailed."

The men and women responsible for the activities of the labor movement in Palestine came here some forty years ago to lay the foundation of what we like to call a labor commonwealth. They came mainly from Eastern Europe, from countries where Jews endured persecution or, at best, existed on sufferance. It was the generation described by the Hebrew poet Bialik in a famous poem written after a wave of pogroms in czarist Russia. He expressed his anguish over Jewish helplessness in life and death:

I grieve for you, my children, my heart is sad for you,
Your dead are vainly dead and neither I nor you
Know why you died or wherefore, nor for whom,
Even as was your life, so senseless was your doom.

This generation decided that the senseless living and sense-less dying of Jews must end. It was they who understood the essence of Zionism—its protest against such a debased existence. The pioneers chose to come to Palestine. Other countries in the world were open to Jews, but they came to Palestine because they believed then, as they believe now, as millions of Jews believe, that the only solution for the senselessness of Jewish life and Jewish death lay in the creation of an independent Jewish life in the Jewish homeland.

The pioneer generation had still another purpose in coming here. They had two goals which inevitably shaped themselves into one. Their second aim was the creation of a new society built on the bases of equality, justice, and cooperation. When they arrived here, they were faced with tough realities. Their mission was to conquer not their fellowmen, but a harsh natural environment, marshes, deserts, the malaria-bearing mosquito. They had also to conquer themselves for these young people were not accustomed to physical labor. They had no experience of a society based on principles of cooperation. They had to overcome much within themselves in order to devote themselves to physical labor, to agriculture, and to the making of a coopera-tive society.

From the outset they sought to achieve these goals in com-plete friendship and cooperation with the Arab population and with Arab laborers. It is significant that the first organization of Arab labor in this country was founded by the Jewish workers who came at that time.

Since 1919, from the formation of the Railway Workers Union, the Histadrut and the labor movement in Palestine have never abandoned concrete attempts for cooperation and contact with our Arab comrades in labor. This was not easy. We have no record of uniform success, but we believe that some of the seeds that we planted during this long period have taken root in spite of all those who opposed such cooperation.

The accomplishments of the labor movement in the villages and towns, in industry and in agriculture were due mainly to two factors: First, these young Jews who wanted to live a life of dignity felt that they had no alternative; they had come here to make a success of it. Another factor was their unlimited faith in man. Throughout these years, in spite of all the obstacles that were put in our way, never did the members of the labor movement, or the young generation trained by the labor movement, give up the hope that humanity and all progressive people would realize the justice of our cause.

From the very beginning of the labor movement in Palestine, we were in close contact with the international labor movement, with the British Labor Party and Trades Union Congress in England and with the labor federations in the United States. We believed in these organizations, in their programs and policies, and we were certain that they, above all, in moral sympathy with our purpose, would help us.

Probably one of the greatest factors in helping us to overcome our initial difficulties was the fact that from the very first, since 1917, we constantly received encouragement from the British labor movement and in later years from the American labor movement. Perhaps that is why the blow that we have lately suffered [the anti-Zionist attitude of the British Labor government under Bevin] has been felt most keenly by the labor movement—even more keenly, if that is possible, than by other sectors of the community. Must we conclude that even those we believed in—those in whose hands it lies to bring about a happier and juster world—do not understand our cause and what we are doing?

As I have said, we came to Palestine to do away with the helplessness of the Jewish people through our own endeavors. Therefore, you will realize what it meant for us to watch from here millions of Jews being slaughtered during these years of war. You have seen Hitler's slaughterhouses, and I will say nothing about them. But you can imagine what it meant to us to sit here with the curse of helplessness again upon us; we could not save them. We were prepared to do so. There was nothing that we were not ready to share with Hitler's victims.

Several times at these hearings we were asked about the wages of labor and if the Jewish labor movement were prepared to make sacrifices for a large Jewish immigration. I am authorized on behalf of the close to 160,000 members of our federation, the Histadrut, to state here in the clearest terms that there is nothing that Jewish labor is not prepared to do in this country in order to receive large masses of Jewish immigrants, with no limitations and with no conditions whatsoever. That is the purpose for which we came; otherwise, our life here too becomes senseless. Need I explain what it meant to us to be only a short distance away from the *Struma* [a ship with "illegal" immigrants], to see hundreds of Jews who had fled for their lives go down to the depths of the sea while we here were unable to save them.

We have many grievances against the government. We have grievances because the government did not help us, as it should have, to establish a sound Arab-Jewish relationship among workers. (We can bring evidence of obstructionism on the part of the government.) We also have grievances because the government did not contribute its share in aiding the social welfare, educational, and medical institutions that we established.

We have taken great burdens upon our shoulders; sometimes it seems that the government has perversely punished us for assuming such responsibilities. Government has practically shirked its duties as far as our labor population is concerned. These are among our grievances. But our chief accusation against government and its White Paper policy is that it forced us to sit here helplessly at a time when we were convinced that we could have rescued not millions but probably hundreds of thousands of Jews. We are convinced that due to this government policy, Jews went to their deaths because they were not allowed to enter the one country where they could have been saved.

Perhaps, gentlemen, this will help you understand the young people that you saw in the DP camps. History repeats itself once again: Jews are with their backs against the wall with no alternative, and these young men, like those who came to Palestine forty years ago, find themselves with only one way before them—to reach Palestine so that their lives may have reason, and so that if they die, their deaths will have reason, too.

In this country we have not overcome all the difficulties before us. There are still deserts, marshes, and misunderstandings. Nevertheless, these young people in the DP camps realize, as we have for decades, that there is no other road.

I don't know, gentlemen, whether you who have the good fortune to belong to the two great democratic nations, the British and the American, can, with the best of will to understand our problems, realize what it means to be the member of a people whose very right to exist is constantly being questioned: our right to be Jews such as we are, no better, but no worse than others in this world, with our own language, our culture, with the right of self-determination and with a readiness to dwell in friendship and cooperation with those near us and those far away. Together with the young and the old survivors in the DP camps, the Jewish workers in this country have decided to do away with this helplessness and dependence upon others within our generation. We Jews only want that which is given naturally to all peoples of the world, to be masters of our own fate—only of our fate, not of the destiny of others; to live as of right and not on sufferance, to have the chance to bring the surviving Jewish children, of whom not so many are now left in the world, to this country so that they may grow up like our youngsters who were born here, free of fear, with heads high. Our children here don't understand why the very existence of the Jewish people as such is questioned. For them, at last, it is natural to be a Jew.

We are certain that given an opportunity of bringing in large masses of Jews into this country, of opening the doors of Palestine to all Jews who wish to come here, we can go on building upon the foundation laid by the labor movement and create a free Jewish society built on the basis of cooperation, equality, and mutual aid. We wish to build such a society not only within the Jewish community, but especially together with those living with us in this country and with all our neighbors. We claim to be no better but surely no worse than other peoples. We hope that with the efforts we have already made in Palestine and will continue to make we, too, will contribute to the welfare of the world and to the creation of that better social order which we all undoubtedly seek.

6. Why We Need a Jewish State

This statement was made at the Twenty-second Zionist Congress in Basel, the first Zionist Congress to convene since the conclusion of World War II. Formerly an opponent of partition, Mrs. Meir came out for a Jewish state as the only solution to the problems created by the Holocaust. (In Yiddish, December, 1946)

The present Labor government of Great Britain refuses to implement resolutions passed and promises made at conventions of the Labor Party over the past thirty years. These British politicians see no need to honor pledges made not only to us, but to millions of British workers and soldiers and to the British people. Now, after the war, we witness deeds committed in Palestine unusual even in our history, replete as it is with cruel decrees. Instead of freedom—suppression; instead of preparation for a Jewish state in Palestine—the expulsion of Jews from the country.

We see how Jews are killed near the shore, on the border of Palestine, by British soldiers, men who had been mobilized not for war with Jewish immigrants, but sent by their nation to fight Hitler and not the Jews. This government, instead of helping us to lay the foundation for a Jewish state and Jewish independence in Palestine, is trying to deprive us of what little independence, what little administrative authority we have laboriously achieved by our own energy.

Why are we now pressing our demand for a Jewish state? When did it become clear to us that we must have absolute control over our lives and immigration, that this must be in the hands of Jews not as a distant aim, but as a desperate, immediate need? We understood this necessity the moment that we, 600,000 Jews in Palestine, despite all that we had created in the country and endured during the long years of war, stood powerless to rescue hundreds and thousands of Jews, perhaps millions, from certain death. The only obstacle between our readiness to rescue the Jews of Europe and the terrible certainty that death awaited them at Hitler's hands, the only thing that blocked their way from death to life, was a political regulation laid down by strangers—the White Paper! The British government stood between us and millions of Jews lost in Europe. Various excuses were found to explain to us why it was impossible to rescue Jews: There was "a lack of ships" to bring Jews ("Was there not a war going on and was it not necessary to transport troops?"). We heard many replies to the question of why Jewish children could not be brought to Palestine. But ships were found to transport Jews from Palestine far away to Mauritius—for that there was no hindrance. In the moments when the *Struma* sank on our shores, when hundreds of Jews were lost practically within our very sight, and we the Jewish Yishuv, who felt ourselves during the war to be the nerve center of European Jewry in all its torments, could be of no help because this White Paper stood as an iron wall between us and the victims of Hitler, when Palestine youth were straining to reach the Jews in the ghettos, to be with them, to unite them and prepare them to revolt, and we could not do this except with the consent of others, when our helplessness was so tragically revealed to us, then the argument among us about the goals of Zionism ceased. Zionism, redemption, and rescue coalesced into one concept; if there are no Jews, there is no redemption; if there is to be redemption, a free Jewish people, Jews must first be rescued from death and destruction and brought to Palestine.

During the war years it became evident to us that no foreign government would bring Jews to Palestine, that no government would feel the agony as we feel it, and that no government would long to save Jews and rescue Jewish lives as we long to do. It is therefore impossible for us to go on in this manner and acquiesce in the fact that our desire to rescue, to build, and to bring Jews to Palestine should be entirely dependent on outsiders. And it became obvious to us that a state was a necessity for us not as a last resort but as an immediate instrument for the rescue of Jews and the upbuilding of Palestine. We must become the masters of our undertaking. Only then will we be able to accomplish whatever is vital to the life of the Jewish people without begging the indulgence of others and as we deem fit.

I will not dwell at length over what we went through in Palestine during the war years. We wanted with all our heart to participate in the war. We claimed that the fight concerned us first and foremost, for it was on us that it was first declared. As long as the war was only against the Jews, we stood alone, without allies; however, once the war embraced the entire world and we wanted to join and fight with all our strength, a long and dolorous chapter commenced. Finally, our youth breached the wall and won the right to go to the front as a Jewish unit. Imagine for yourselves what we went through before permission was granted for a few dozens of our comrades to be dropped as parachutists behind the lines in the occupied countries, there to contact the Jews, bring tidings of Palestine, encourage them, and assist them to rebel against the conquerors; consider what we in Palestine felt when we were forced to seek all manner of stratagems to provide what little help we could to Jews in the charnelhouse of Eastern Europe!

During the war we were also afforded an insight into the nature of a government which is indifferent to the interests of the people it governs. The economic regime in Palestine during the war was such as to indicate that the government cared nothing for the welfare of the Palestine economy or whether it emerged from the war strong and healthy and able to com-

pete with other countries. We often suspected—and let us not
be accused of exaggerating!—that the government's economic
system was designed so that Palestine should not be on a com-
petitive footing.

At every turn—ranging from the crucial task of saving Jewish
lives to lesser matters such as maintaining a healthy economy so
that we might be able to absorb a large immigration—it became
clear to us daily that the only way of fulfilling Zionism in the
present situation was a Jewish state. The fact that the Zionist
movement and the Jewish people found the courage during the
war years to declare openly that in Jewry's present situation
there was only one solution to the Jewish question—the establishment of a Jewish state—was one of the few rays of light
in the dark days of war; and not only for us and American
Jewry, but—more important—for Jews in the ghettos and
forests.

We had truly hoped that a better world would emerge when
the war was over, and that then the rights of the Jewish people
would be recognized. This did not happen. Instead, the British
government began to make declarations "proving" that a schism
existed among Jews. Bevin set out to divide the Jews into
Zionists and non-Zionists, extremists and nonextremists. Thereafter he started dividing the Jews into those who wished to
immigrate to Palestine and those who had no such wish. When
the British government and the Palestine government proceeded
to explain the outrageous actions of June 29, against the elected
representatives of the Jewish community of Palestine, they announced that everything which took place that day was actually
aimed against the extremists, whereas no harm would befall
decent people. On that Saturday morning, at seven thirty, we
heard on the radio from the high commissioner that the entire
Yishuv (the Jewish community) could sit back quietly: Moderate
and decent Jews would not be harmed. Action was being taken
only against a few extremist and harmful individuals of the Jewish Agency, the National Executive, the Executive Committee of
the Histadrut Workers' Federation, and some thirty settlements

throughout the country. Other than these "handfuls," the entire Yishuv were decent people who had nothing to fear; no one would harm them.

Once the British government embarked on this path, the Yishuv was faced with two options: either to tell Bevin and his colleagues in the Cabinet: "You were right, there is such a division, and by following this path you may possibly accomplish what you want," or to speak decisively: "The Jewish people, the Yishuv, the Zionist movement are one in their aims."

Our Zionist friends living afar may possibly allow themselves to exaggerate the strength of the Yishuv in Palestine; we do not, of course, wish to be belittled, but we must beware of exaggerating the extent of our strength. We, the Palestinians, unfortunately cannot permit ourselves the luxury of fantasy. We must calculate our strength with detachment. Nevertheless, we decided to muster all our capacity and do two things simultaneously: first, to continue our building in Palestine without pause; second, to convince England that the Yishuv would fight any attempt to submit the issue of our settlement in Palestine to the will of another people who would not permit us to bring Jews into Palestine in accordance with the need of the Jews and the absorption capacity of the country. We would accept no decree stifling our growth.

When the Jewish survivors in the DP camps were asked whether they wished to go to America, to Australia, or to other countries, it might well have been natural for these tortured souls, remnants not only of the Jewish people but of families, communities, and entire countries, to have instantly grasped such offers with open arms. Yet these Jews—in DP camp after camp—replied as one: "Let there be an end to our worldwide wandering. We have but one home—Palestine!"

I do not know if the Zionist world and the Jewish world are aware of what it meant to us that these few Jews have survived not only for themselves, but for us as well. The primary thing is that they have survived, and the second—that having survived, they were aware of what the present time required of them and of what Zionism means today in the life of the Jews! That is a miracle.

And we have witnessed another miracle—the reaction of our sabras, boys and girls born in Palestine, who knew nothing of the Diaspora and had very rarely seen Diaspora Jews with the exception of those who had come to Palestine—a youth who had no memory of the Jewish *stetl* with its tribulations, traditions, and marvelous Jewish life. Our sabras, growing up in Palestine erect and confident, were ready to sacrifice themselves without fear for European Jewry. From time to time we used to ask ourselves anxiously: What is to bind these children of ours to the Jewish people, the major portion of whom is still abroad? The time came when the sabras themselves gave the answer. These young people are strangers to casuistry and abstract precepts; they are plain and pure as the sun of Palestine. For them, matters are simple, clear, and uncomplicated. When the catastrophe descended upon the Jews of the world, and Jews began coming to Palestine in "illegal" ships, as they still do, we saw these children of ours go down to the seas and at risk to their lives—this is no rhetoric, but literally so—ford the waves to reach the boats and bear these Jews ashore on their shoulders. This, too, is no rhetoric, no flowery speech, but the literal truth: sixteen- and eighteen-year-old Palestinian girls and boys carried the survivors on their backs. From the mouths of Jews borne on their shoulders I have heard that they shed tears for the first time, after all they had been through in Europe for seven years, on seeing a Palestinian youth bearing grown men and women to the soil of the homeland. We have been blessed in this youth, which makes no account of the degree of danger or self-sacrifice, but simply, with a sure dedication, sets out to offer its life not in behalf of its own particular kibbutz, or of the Yishuv in Palestine in general, but for the sake of every Jewish child or old man seeking entry.

Since the British government has terminated immigration by certificate, the path leading Jews to Palestine will have to be independent of the British government's permits; if Jews are not given certificates, they will immigrate to Palestine without permits, and they so immigrate! Theirs is no easy path. However, Jews are prepared to embark in the "illegal" ships despite their knowledge that immigration to Palestine means that they will arrive off the coast of Haifa, where they will be met by troops who will shower blows and gas bombs on them; some of them will be killed, and those killed will not even be brought to Jewish burial. If they are lucky, they will have the privilege of being led to a fresh detention camp in Cyprus! Notwithstanding all this, Jews set out—young and old—and children are born in the terrible boats. As I have said before, this is one miracle. The other miracle is that the youth of Palestine is doing its utmost in the struggle on their behalf.

Free Jewish immigration into Palestine does not depend on the British government, but on the Jews themselves and on Zionists throughout the world. Our chief demand at present concerns immigration—that it should increase, that ever more ships should come, that many thousands of survivors should come to Palestine every month. And while the British government is engaged in debating for a year about immigration certificates for 100,000 Jews, we must transform this matter in short order into an accomplished fact. We must transport the 100,000 Jews to Palestine in our own ships, and bring them in with our own means.

The twenty-ninth of June, when the British government arrested the leaders of the Yishuv, was a turning point in Palestine. In this action the government overreached itself. It is not true, that searches for arms commenced on the twenty-ninth of June or that this was the government's response to various Haganah acts performed in Palestine before that date. Palestinians and non-Palestinians alike remember Ramat Hakovesh and Hulda, when the British started searching for arms among us. At Ramat Hakovesh the British came to search for arms shortly after the disturbances in which members of this settlement fell almost daily. On the twenty-ninth of June the government set out to break the spirit and backbone of the Yishuv in Palestine by one concentrated blow. That day the government fell upon us; the troops it sent against us assaulted the Jewish Agency building, occupied it, and held it for a week; that day, on a Saturday morning, the members of the Executive and of the National Council were led off as prisoners; in one morning the British occupied dozens of settlements and attempted forcibly to confiscate the arms which the government well knew were essential for our defense. In one day they filled detention camps with close to 4,000 Jewish prisoners. In doing all this, the government sought to break the fighting spirit of the Yishuv in Palestine. By its actions, the government wished to smash whatever independence the Jews had acquired in Palestine. In taking the Agency building, it proposed to manifest to all that the Jews were deluding themselves in believing that they were independent and could elect leaders of their own choice.

It was not long before the government realized its ignominious defeat. Though there might have been differences of opinion about tactics in the Yishuv, sound Jewish political sense dictated that when the hand of strangers was raised against our independence, Jews would draw tightly together. Above all, these blows strengthened our determination to demand that full measure of political independence which can be attained only through the establishment of a Jewish state.

7. The SS *Exodus 1947*

The most dramatic episode in the saga of "illegal" immigration to Palestine was that of the SS Exodus 1947. Over four thousand Jews from displaced persons camps in Germany were brought to the French port of Sète from which they embarked for Palestine. On July 18 Exodus 1947 was attacked and boarded by the British. Contrary to their previous practice of sending captured refugees to nearby detention camps in Cyprus, the British sent the refugees back to France. The French refused to force the refugees to leave the ship. The British then sent the Jewish survivors of the concentration camps to Hamburg, where they arrived on September 8.

Mrs. Meir's statement to the National Council of Jewish Palestine was made a number of days before the final destination of the SS Exodus 1947 was definitely known. (In Hebrew, August 26, 1947)

There is almost nothing left to say about this ship which dramatically symbolizes the state not only of the Jewish people, but of the entire world as well. What has been happening these past weeks, ever since *Exodus 1947* reached the shore of Palestine and earlier, when the boat still stood outside Palestine's territorial waters, could not have taken place had not the world, after its victory over Hitler, continued to liv in the moral climate created by Hitler. Most shocking, perhaps, is not what happened to the thousands in the boats, the infants, the pregnant women, the young and old. Even more shocking is the fact that not a single country, no statesman cried out in bitter protest against a world in which such events can take place. We have not yet heard of individuals other than Jews who joined in our fast for the men and women on the *Exodus*. And let wise men not tell us that neither heaven nor earth is moved by a fast. Every one of us is well aware that in our world a fast by Jews is no earth-shaking event. Nevertheless, it would have been fitting for some Gentiles—men of letters, clergymen, statesmen, educators, writers, artists—in some corner of the world to have fasted with us, not for our sake, but for the sake of their own conscience. If such there were, we have not heard of them.

We know that on this ship there are dozens of expectant mothers near their time and women a few days after childbirth, as well as infants born on board. From correspondents permitted to board the boat we have heard of the conditions in which these mothers and infants exist. Where are the women's organizations of the world who are always engaged in fighting for justice? Why do we not hear their voices protesting against this iniquity to mothers, newborn infants, and children still unborn? Not a single voice of theirs has been heard. This shames the whole world!

Yet our people exist in this world, and in this world we must fight for the minimum of justice which is our due. I doubt whether any other people would have had the courage to continue the struggle under such conditions and against such odds. Had the Jewish people had a choice, it might perhaps have despaired. However, since we have no alternative and are persuaded of the justice of our cause, Jews go on fighting despite everything. To others it may seem strange that the Jewish people is still convinced of eventual victory.

The British government will not succeed in concealing a primary and fundamental fact—namely, that this ship was attacked *outside Palestine's territorial waters*. The British government cannot succeed in its attempt to hide the truth because all the facts on hand prove that the ship was attacked outside Palestine's territorial waters, contrary to all international law; attacked with such force that it is a miracle that the boat succeeded in reaching the shores of Palestine. In our particular situation, the evidence of Jews is disregarded; what Jews testify has no significance in the eyes of the British government. Any Jew, or Zionist, or member of the Jewish Agency, or of any Jewish institution is disqualified a priori. But on this ship there was also a non-Jew, a non-Zionist, not a member of the Jewish Agency Executive. On board was a perfectly worthy Gentile—a priest. He made the voyage with the Jews from the beginning to the end. This priest has already given much information and has more to tell.

There were dead on board when the ship reached our shores; the British government observes one rule: It permits freedom of entry to Palestine for a dead Jew. A dead Jew may enter the country and be buried in it, legally. He is not imprisoned as an "illegal." The government brings him in at its own expense and in its great munificence does not deduct the corpse from our quota of immigration certificates. A net gain! But only a Jew murdered by a British bullet may benefit from this privilege. Any Jew reaching the shores of Palestine alive is sentenced to deportation. He has transgressed the law, so upon his arrival in Palestine a fresh chapter of torture commences for him. The sentence is deportation, and the British government from time to time considers how best to make these Jews suffer. Life in a detention camp in Palestine, in Atlit, is not harsh enough. Deportation to Cyprus, to a new prison camp, with crowded quarters, insufficient water, enforced idleness so that all sense of purpose in living is lost by Hitler's survivors, is not penalty enough. So a fresh method has been devised—deportation back to Germany. For a brief while the British government toyed with the hope that it would not remain alone in its holy war against the Jews and that it would be joined by another nation —the French people. A day or two before the arrival of the boats off the shores of France, British government circles stated that their action had been taken in total agreement with the French government. But observe France's attitude! They did not insist on the debarkation of the "illegals" at their ports. This was no doubt a bitter disappointment for Britain.

In the days immediately following the deportation, an attempt was made to explain to us that it was impossible to send the *Exodus* immigrants to Cyprus because there was no housing there for 4,000 Jews. Yet, lo and behold, the latest British government communiqué states explicitly that in the territories at the disposal of the British authorities—aside from the British zone in Germany—there are only two places where both housing and provision are available—namely, Cyprus and Palestine. Both these places are disqualified, however, since they are desired by the survivors—Cyprus as an eventual stepping-stone to Palestine. There is only one other place under British rule where the people can be housed and maintained, a place of unqualified torment for Jewish survivors and therefore the chosen place—namely, the soil of Germany.

Nothing we have done since *Exodus 1947* reached the shores of Palestine, none of the actions taken here by the Jewish Agency and the National Council, by the entire Yishuv, and by the Jewish Agency Executive in London, have availed us. The activities of Jewish institutions throughout Europe and in Washington have not helped. The British government could not be restrained from issuing its communiqué bidding that *Exodus* be returned to Europe.

Apparently those responsible for this evil policy are unable to forgive us one thing: that we are not a passive herd. Why do we presume to act as a nation even before securing the British government's agreement thereto? How do we dare to elect administrative bodies, accept their authority, and behave like an organized and disciplined people? Why do we not think only of our own advantage and obey the pronouncements of His Majesty's Foreign Secretary? Why does each of us live according to his own judgment? They will not forgive us this. They cannot grasp, or in their folly do not wish to understand, that the whole problem of the hundreds of thousands of surviving Jews in Europe—both in the DP camps and elsewhere—was not created for the sole purpose of making trouble for the British government. "The Jews have it wonderfully well in these places; they lack nothing," we are told.

From a recent British communiqué we learn that the entire labor of bringing Jews to Palestine is a Zionist conspiracy for political purposes. The British do not wish to understand that Jews cannot continue to live in the DP camps. How can they pretend that it is neither necessary nor desirable to depart from these camps two years after the end of the war? What is so surprising about the fact that the Jewish Yishuv here believes that the single, overriding purpose of its existence lies in its obligation to rescue every Jew possible and bring him here? No Jew possessed of national consciousness and understanding will observe any edict opposed to Jewish immigration to Palestine. Why cannot these British Cabinet ministers absorb the plain fact that it is the Jewish will to live which commands Jews to remain on their miserable boats and not Zionist threats or propaganda? The campaign now being waged by Britain is not directed against some shrewd propaganda outfit, but against a Jewish community aware that it is conducting a life-or-death struggle. The British government has issued its terrible threats: "Either you disembark in France or else you return to Germany —to that soil saturated with so much Jewish blood." But there is something greater than threats. It is the compulsion to live of mothers who bore their infants on board and are determined to be free women in the homeland and will not disembark anywhere else in the world. Against this even the government is helpless. It can kill both mother and infant; it cannot kill this will. While there is a Jew alive in the world seeking to immigrate to Palestine, the British government will have to employ force to fight him back.

According to the British communiqué, the Jews actually want to go to Germany. For they have an alternative: They can disembark in France. If they do not disembark in France, it is a clear sign that they want to go to Germany. The communiqué further states that if the Jewish Agency were really concerned for the welfare of the Jews, it would send an emissary posthaste to advise the Jews to benefit from the generosity of the British government; they should be urged to disembark in a French port and proceed to a new Diaspora. So much for the moral stance and the comprehension of the British.

We have long maintained that Britain's right to her presence in this country derived from one single document—the mandate. She undertook to implement the mandate, as well as to help in Jewish immigration, Jewish settlement, and the return of the Jews to the homeland—to their national home. By publishing the White Paper, Britain abrogated the mandate, and having done so, she shed this responsibility. And if there were need for signal proof that Britain lacked the moral—aside from the legal—right to rule in Palestine, this has been provided by the immigration issue. The communiqué "explains" why Jews are no longer sent to Cyprus: because the scheme was a failure; because despite detention in Cyprus, Jews continued to come. The British hope that through deportation of the *Exodus 1947* they will succeed in frightening the Jews of the DP camps and terrify us. There can be only one answer on our part: This flow of boats will not cease. I am aware that the Jews seeking to immigrate to Palestine and those assisting them are now facing terrible difficulties, with all the forces of the British Empire concentrated for one purpose: to attack these creaking boats laden with human suffering. Nevertheless, I believe that there can be only one effective answer: the uninterrupted flow of the "illegal" ships. I have no doubts about the stand of the Jews of the camps; they are ready for all perils in order to leave the camps. The Jewish survivors of many European countries cannot remain where they are. If we in Palestine together with American, South African, and British Jewry do not let ourselves be frightened, the boats will continue to come. With much travail, greater than in the past—but come they will. I do not for one moment disregard what the thousands on these boats will face in the coming days. I know that each one of us would deem himself happy if he could be with them. Every one of us worries over what may happen when the Jews on the *Exodus* are brought to Germany, without the French government to stand by them, and with the British forces completely free to teach these lawbreakers a lesson. There can be no doubt that they will be steadfast, as they have been until now. The question is only whether there is no hope for some last-minute change of heart on the part of the British.

Since we are incapable of despair, we wish at this moment, from this place, once more to address our call to the world, to the nations—to the many who suffered no little during the war, to those on many of whose fronts Jews fought and helped in their liberation. To these nations we issue this last-minute appeal. Is it possible that no voice will be raised, that the British government will not be told: Remove the whip and the rifle from over the heads of the Jews on the *Exodus*? And to Britain we must say: It is a great illusion to believe us to be weak! Let Great Britain with her mighty fleet and her many guns and planes know that this people is not so weak and that its strength will yet stand it in good stead to withstand this assault as well!

Every one of us must help in bringing Jews to Palestine. Whoever is able to aid these Jews in reaching Palestine, by any means, of them it shall be said: Blessed are they! Holy in our eyes are these youths of Israel, the Palestinians, the Americans —who risk their lives to bring in mother and child to Palestine. Britain must be made aware that every Jew will do his share; perhaps if she understands this, she will reconsider her purpose. If she does not do so, she will confront the Jewish people everywhere; in the camps, in Cyprus, in the Yishuv, in America —wherever there are Jews. She will confront Jews, who know only one thing: that their existence depends on the right of Jews to enter their homeland. Since this is what we all seek, and we have no other way, they will come.

8. In the Midst of Battle: 1948

In January, 1948, the fortunes of the 600,000 Jews in Palestine were at low ebb because of concerted Arab attacks and lack of weapons. Mrs. Meir, then comparatively unknown outside Palestine, flew to the United States to raise funds for needed arms. She made an unscheduled appearance before the Council of Jewish Federations in Chicago. Her extemporaneous statement electrified American Jewry and altered its scale of giving. (In English, January 21, 1948)

Ben-Gurion described the result of her mission: "Someday when history will be written, it will be said that there was a Jewish woman who got the money which made the state possible."

I have had the privilege of representing Palestine Jewry in this country and in other countries when the problems that we faced were those of building more kibbutzim, of bringing in more Jews in spite of political obstacles and Arab riots. We always had faith that in the end we would win, that everything we were doing in the country led to the independence of the Jewish people and to a Jewish state.

Long before we had dared pronounce that word, we knew what was in store for us. Today we have reached a point when the nations of the world have given us their decision—the establishment of a Jewish state in a part of Palestine. Now in Palestine we are fighting to make this resolution of the United Nations a reality, not because we wanted to fight. If we had the choice, we would have chosen peace to build in peace.

Friends, we have no alternative in Palestine. The Mufti and his men have declared war upon us. We have to fight for our lives, for our safety, and for what we have accomplished in Palestine, and perhaps above all, we must fight for Jewish honor and Jewish independence.

Without exaggeration, I can tell you that the Jewish community in Palestine is doing this well. Many of you have visited Palestine; all of you have read about our young people and have a notion as to what our youth is like. I have known this generation for the last twenty-seven years. I thought I knew them. I realize now that even I did not.

These young boys and girls, many in their teens, are bearing the burden of what is happening in the country with a spirit that no words can describe. You see these youngsters in open cars—not armored cars—in convoys going from Tel Aviv to Jerusalem, knowing that every time they start out from Tel Aviv or from Jerusalem there are probably Arabs behind the orange groves or the hills, waiting to ambush the convoy. Despite the danger the British government gives no military escort to the civilian convoys. These boys and girls have accepted the task of bringing Jews over these roads in safety as naturally as though they were going out to their daily work or to their classes in the university.

We must ask the Jews the world over to see us as the front line and do for us what the United States did for England when England was in the front line in the World War. All we ask of Jews the world over, and mainly of the Jews in the United States, is to give us the possibility of going on with the struggle.

When the trouble started, we asked young people from the age of seventeen to twenty-five who were not members of Haganah, to volunteer. Up to the day that I left home on Thursday morning, when the registration of this age group was still going on, over 20,000 young men and women had signed up. As of now we have about 9,000 people mobilized in the various parts of the country. We must triple this number within the next few days.

We have to maintain these men. No government sends its soldiers to the front and expects them to take along from their homes the most elementary requirements—blankets, bedding, clothing. A people that is fighting for its very life knows how to supply the men they send to the front lines. We too must do the same.

Thirty-five of our boys, unable to go by car on the road to besieged Kfar Etzion to bring help, set out by foot through the hills; they knew the road, the Arab villages on that road, and the danger they would have to face. Some of the finest youngsters we have in the country were in that group, and they were all killed, every one of them. We have a description from an Arab of how they fought to the end for over seven hours against hundreds of Arabs. According to this Arab, the last boy killed, with no more ammunition left, died with a stone in his hand.

I want to say to you, friends, that the Jewish community in Palestine is going to fight to the very end. If we have arms to fight with, we will fight with those, and if not, we will fight with stones in our hands.

I want you to believe me when I say that I came on this special mission to the United States today not to save 700,000 Jews. During the last few years the Jewish people lost 6,000,000 Jews, and it would be audacity on our part to worry the Jewish people throughout the world because a few hundred thousand more Jews were in danger.

That is not the issue. The issue is that if these 700,000 Jews in Palestine can remain alive, then the Jewish people as such is alive and Jewish independence is assured. If these 700,000 people are killed off, then for many centuries, we are through with this dream of a Jewish people and a Jewish homeland.

My friends, we are at war. There is no Jew in Palestine who does not believe that finally we will be victorious. That is the spirit of the country. We have known Arab riots since 1921 and '29 and '36. We know what happened to the Jews of Europe during this last war. And every Jew in the country also knows that within a few months a Jewish state in Palestine will be established. We knew that the price we would have to pay would be the best of our people. There are over 300 killed by now. There will be more. There is no doubt that there will be more. But there is also no doubt that the spirit of our young people is such that no matter how many Arabs invade the country, their spirit will not falter.

However, this valiant spirit alone cannot face rifles and machine guns. Rifles and machine guns without spirit are not worth very much, but spirit without arms can in time be broken with the body.

Our problem is time. The time factor is now the most important. Millions of dollars that we may get in three or four months will mean very little in deciding the present issue. The question is what can we get immediately. And, my friends, when I say immediately, this does not mean next month. It does not mean two months from now. It means now.

Much must be prepared now so that we can hold out. There are unlimited opportunities, but are we going to get the necessary means? Considering myself not as a guest, but as one of you, I say that the question before each one is simply whether the Yishuv, and the youngsters that are in the front line, will have to fail because money that should have reached Palestine today will reach it in a month or two months from now?

Is it possible that time should decide the issue not because Palestinian Jews are cowards, not because they are incapable, but merely because they lack the material means to carry on?

I have come to the United States, and I hope you will understand me if I say that it is not an easy matter for any of us to leave home at present—to my sorrow I am not in the front line. I am not with my daughter in the Negev or with other sons and daughters in the trenches. But I have a job to do.

I have come here to try to impress Jews in the United States with the fact that within a very short period, a couple of weeks, we must have in cash between twenty-five and thirty million dollars. In the next two or three weeks we can establish ourselves. Of that we are convinced, and you must have faith; we are sure that we can carry on.

I said before that the Yishuv will give, is giving of its means. But please remember that even while shooting is going on, we must carry on so that our economy remains intact. Our factories must go on. Our settlements must not be broken up. We know that this battle is being waged for those not yet in the country. There are 30,000 Jews detained right next door to Palestine in Cyprus. I believe that within a very short period, within the next two or three months at most, these 30,000 will be with us, among them thousands of infants and young children. We must now think of preparing means of absorbing them.

We know that within the very near future, hundreds of thousands more will be coming in. We must see that our economy is intact. Of course, security has priority. But I am certain that if you were asked whether we should destroy all that we have established in Palestine to put everything solely in security and then have to face the problem of building our economy anew, you would say "No."

I want you to understand that there is no despair in the Yishuv. This is true not only of the young people. I have traveled the road from Tel Aviv to Jerusalem and other roads quite a bit. I have seen these dangerous buses filled not only with young Haganah men and girls, but with old people traveling the roads as a matter of course.

When you go to Tel Aviv now, you will find the city full of life; only the shooting that you hear on the outskirts of Tel Aviv and Jaffa reminds one that the situation in the country is not normal.

But it would be a crime on my part not to describe the situation to you exactly as it is. Merely with our ten fingers and merely with spirit and sacrifice, we cannot carry on this battle, and the only *hinterland* that we have is you. The Mufti has the Arab states—not all so enthusiastic about helping him but states with government budgets.

The Egyptian government can vote a budget to aid our antagonists. The Syrian government can do the same. We have no governments. But we have millions of Jews in the Diaspora, and exactly as we have faith in our youngsters in Palestine I have faith in Jews in the United States; I believe that they will realize the peril of our situation and will do what they have to do.

I know that we are not asking for something easy. I myself have sometimes been active in various campaigns and fund collections, and I know that collecting at once a sum such as I ask is not simple. But I have seen our people at home. I have seen them come from the offices to the clinics when we called the community to give their blood for a blood bank to treat the wounded. I have seen them lined up for hours, waiting so that some of their blood can be added to this bank. It is blood plus money that is being given in Palestine.

I know that many of you would be as anxious as our people to be on the very front line. I do not doubt that there are many young people among the Jewish community in the United States who would do exactly what our young people are doing in Palestine.

We are not a better breed; we are not the best Jews of the Jewish people. It so happened that we are there and you are here. I am certain that if you were in Palestine and we were in the United States, you would be doing what we are doing there, and you would ask us here to do what you will have to do.

I want to close with paraphrasing one of the greatest speeches that was made during the Second World War—the words of Churchill. I am not exaggerating when I say that the Yishuv in Palestine will fight in the Negev and will fight in Galilee and will fight on the outskirts of Jerusalem until the very end.

You cannot decide whether we should fight or not. We will. The Jewish community in Palestine will raise no white flag for the Mufti. That decision is taken. Nobody can change it. You can only decide one thing: whether we shall be victorious in this fight or whether the Mufti will be victorious. That decision American Jews can make. It has to be made quickly within hours, within days.

And I beg of you—don't be too late. Don't be bitterly sorry

three months from now for what you failed to do today. The time is now.

I have spoken to you without a grain of exaggeration. I have not tried to paint the picture in false colors. It consists of spirit and certainty of our victory on the one hand, and dire necessity for carrying on the battle on the other.

I want to thank you again for having given me the opportunity at a conference that I am certain has a full agenda to say these few words to you. I leave the platform without any doubt in my mind or my heart that the decision that will be taken by American Jewry will be the same as that which was taken by the Jewish community in Palestine, so that within a few months from now we will all be able to participate not only in the joy of resolving to establish a Jewish state, but in the joy of laying the cornerstone of the Jewish state.

9. We Must Close the Gap

As Minister of Labor Mrs. Meir forthrightly attacked tendencies which widened the economic gap between veteran settlers and newcomers. (In Hebrew, July 25, 1950)

We are not concerned merely with the issue of increased production. I must confess that were we debating the question of how soon all the workers of Israel would acquire refrigerators, washing machines, cars, and all manner of good things deserved by every person in the country, I would say: "Let us wait." This "redemption" will not be too late even if it arrives in five years' time. That is not our problem.

The issue before us is simple and cruel; as long as we lack the courage to face it and decide "yes" or "no," unequivocally, we shall not solve it. We must answer the following question: Is there any connection between our talk in favor of immigration and our deeds for such immigration? Let me word it differently: Is there any connection between our talk and our treatment of the immigrant? Are we only for an abstract, collective immigration, numbering 100,000, 200,000, 400,000, or also for the entry of actual, flesh-and-blood immigrants, each an individual?

What path do we propose to follow? Is there a genuine coordination between our talk of immigration and the reality being created in Israel? This reality—let us admit it openly—indicates the emergence of two separate groups within the Jewish population in Israel: one group of so-called old-timers and a second group of new immigrants. At present an abyss exists between these two groups which cannot be bridged by social welfare, be it ever so devoted. Are we following a course that will lead to the closing of this gap or, at least, its gradual diminution? I fear that we are following a course calculated to achieve the reverse.

A few days ago I went on a tour in order to see how we absorb immigrants, how we remove people from the camps, and to note what prospects for better conditions exist. I observed two closely linked situations. I saw what we call *ma'abarot*—tent encampments. And I saw the construction sites where we are supposed to build many hundreds of housing units. In many places this building was not progressing. What was the reason? In Acre, for instance, we are constructing hundreds of housing units for immigrants. When I came there, four men, contractors and laborers, begged me to send them ten skilled workers—four builders, four scaffolding erectors, and two iron benders. "If we get them," they assured, "we shall accomplish two things: (a) we will employ another hundred immigrants"—standing next to me was the director of the Acre Labor Exchange, who told me that he had 180 unemployed on his lists—"(b) there will be tremendous progress in the rate of building."

On this summer day we all suffer from the heat. But I am already suffering from the coming winter; I worry about every warm day that passes and brings us closer to days of rain, storm, and possibly snow. I urge you to go and see for yourselves the tents in Galilee and on the hills of Jerusalem. Yet despite the desperate need, ten expert building workers for Acre, and another ten for Halsa,* and another ten for Beersheba are unobtainable.

I was at a meeting of representatives of all the surrounding settlements at Ayelet Hashahar. We discussed various matters related to the absorption of thousands of immigrant families in Galilee: labor schedules, development projects, public works, and so forth. I discovered that at Halsa they had been unable to

---

* The area on which Kiryat Shmonah is built.

build houses for the past six months. I asked the settlements with skilled workers to send five workmen to Halsa. A member of one of the settlements told me: "We employ building workers from Haifa whom we pay two pounds a day more than they get in Haifa. Pay them a bit more than they receive at my settlement, and they will go to work at Halsa." Since I still respect the worker, I will not accept this counsel.

Only this morning good friends proposed a similar course to me and also suggested that we conscript skilled building workers in order to ensure that the rains will not catch hundreds and thousands of families with children in half-completed buildings without a roof over their heads. Perhaps you can figure out how Yemenite children are to pass a rainy winter in the hills of Galilee? I will not accept such measures.

As I said before, I am not worried about how soon a building worker will get the means to buy a refrigerator. I want to know by what means a Yemenite immigrant family will secure a roof over its head. We have chanted songs, written articles, and listened to fervid speeches about immigrant absorption, but I want to know how a Yemenite family will come anywhere near owning a home and the barest minimum for its existence. How will this small and poor state—postwar and still without peace —find the vast means needed for shelter, food, clothing, and other necessities, including a refrigerator, and at the same time perform the primary task for which alone the state is worth having? I readily confess that I have no need for a Jewish state with a high standard of living but without a large, unlimited, Jewish immigration. I need a Jewish state for one thing only: that the gates of this state should be open without restriction to all Jews who understand what this state means for them and will want to come here in the wake of such understanding.

If we must suffer for this sacred cause, then all of us will suffer: Let us not create two distinct groups of people among us. There are countries in the world where such classes exist. There are even instances of dangerous class distinctions not only between employers and employees, but between employees and employees. In the countries where such "classes" exist, we may be certain that immigration, absorption, and Zionism are not presented as desirable goals.

On my recent visit to the United States my task was to increase the "production" of the material known as dollars so that they might flow to the coffers of the United Jewish Appeal and from there to Israel. The amounts we are now receiving are small and insufficient for our needs. In regard to every single dollar we get we must decide whether it should be used for defense expenditure, or food (in America I said: We live in Israel with the feeling that today's austerity is tomorrow's luxury), or raw material for the factories, or building materials for housing, or for agriculture.

Comrade Dov Joseph,* this relentless man, expends each dollar first on food and raw materials. But what about the building materials? What about the minimum requirements of the immigrants? Is what we manufacture in Israel purchased mainly or in large measure by the new immigrants? Unfortunately, no! The veteran settlers, the privileged group living in Israel, now consider standard furniture neither good enough nor attractive enough; better products must be manufactured for us. Today the raw material for such manufacture is provided at the direct expense of the Yemenite or Iraqi immigrant family. On whose behalf did we demand this money? Not on behalf of the established settlers. On the contrary, we always declared proudly that we required nothing. "The Yemenite and Iraqi Jews are your Jews just as they are ours. You must undertake a major share of this burden." But I am gradually reaching the horrible conviction that this is not the truth. The dollars we receive are consumed by us, because our standard of living is higher, because our demands are greater. We silence our conscience by the explanation that we are accustomed to more than an immigrant who comes from the Yemen or Iraq. But why do we require more than they?

If a large share of the dollars we consume were at least reimbursed by dollars we bring into the country through our exports

---

* Then Minister of Supply and Rationing.

and not merely by the dollars donated, the situation would be different. But our own work brings in no dollars. Believe me, I have no special love for the dollar rather than for any other currency. It is not my fault that this world is so arranged that purchases must be paid for in dollars, and not only in America, but in East and West, in Czechoslovakia and in Holland, in the Soviet Union as well as in the United States.

How do we, the veterans in Israel, become self-supporting? How do we change our production methods so that we can earn some dollars? I do not pretend to understand economics, but some things may be understood without expertise in this branch of knowledge. Ignorance of economics is no valid excuse for failing to face an unpalatable fact: There is no formula for bringing dollars into the country without increasing export and without producing for export. As long as there is no such marvelous formula, we have no choice but to manufacture products under such conditions and at such prices as will induce the world to buy our exports in amounts large enough to enable us to buy what we need without consuming funds that properly should be expended on immigrants. I am prepared to trudge not only from meeting to meeting, but also from house to house, to make all aware that whatever they do—sitting down to table, wearing clothes, furbishing their home, favoring their children—is done at the immigrants' expense. Can we enjoy life with this knowledge?

True, labor alone cannot solve this problem. But I am not interested at the moment in analyzing whether the employers do or do not want increased production. I can assume that they do not want it, and I can essay an explanation as to the reason. But this is irrelevant. Have there been any important objectives desired by the workers which they failed to achieve? I know of none. Did everybody want a state? No. The principal element wanting the state was the labor community. Whenever the majority of the labor community wanted something, they knew how to attain it. When, as our sabras say, "they really really wanted," they succeeded. We wanted to bring in immigrants by every method. Did everyone want this? No. But when our youth and our workers realized that this was the essence of Zionism and the meaning of their lives, they brought in the immigrants. Of course, we made sacrifices and endured hardships. But what was ever vouchsafed us with ease? Did the employers in this country want a Histadrut? We wanted it and built it into a vast economic force. Did the employers want Solel Boneh, Mekorot, the housing companies, Hamashbir, Tnuva,* the cooperatives and all our institutions to develop in so spectacular a fashion? We wanted it. And so it was. In the matter of the immigrants, too, *we must want*. If we, the labor community, understand the shame and tragedy of our present way of life, if we realize that in the long run no immigrants will be absorbed by merely talk of immigration, the solution will depend primarily on us.

Has the labor community abandoned the absorption of new immigrants into the framework of the society we wish to build? Will this society of workers in Israel be one solely for a special breed of "aristocrats," for those who managed to arrive here ten to fifteen years ago and perhaps for some who entered the country five years ago? In the school known as the Histadrut, the community of workers in Israel, we all learned that not enthusiastic speech but implementation is important. I know how carefully the oldest of our comrades weighed the words they uttered when they spoke of fundamental matters, lest they pretend to more than they could really do, for the cardinal precept was action. Though it may be slightly "old-fashioned," perhaps we should return to those concepts. The workers' movement, the wonderfully strong and visionary organization of the Histadrut, will then revert to its beginnings, and we will undertake afresh our present duty: to implement the goal of proper immigrant absorption.

---

* Solel, Boneh, Mekorot, Hamashbir, Tnuva—economic agencies of the Histadrut, the Israel General Federation of Labor.

10. On National Insurance

Mrs. Meir, then Minister of Labor, introduced the first National Insurance Bill to the Knesset. (In Hebrew, January 5, 1952)

It is a momentous occasion for any state when its legislative body opens its debate on a social insurance bill. May I be allowed to say that for our young country such an event is of seven-fold magnitude. It is a great privilege for the Knesset that in the fourth year of our existence it is already preparing to debate this bill which comprises the first stage of a comprehensive social insurance plan.

The aspiration for a just human society has characterized the Jewish people from its first appearance on the stage of history and inspired its prophets to fight for the cause of the poor and the widowed. These visions have left their imprint on the cultural development of mankind.

Those who formulated the basic principles of Zionism and those who laid down the foundations on which the State of Israel rests linked political renaissance with the principles of social justice.

The tenets of mutual aid and help for the needy were established at the very beginning of the workers' movement in Israel. They became the cornerstone on which the Histadrut was founded. During the long rule of the mandatory regime, which ignored the basic needs of the Jewish Yishuv, the Histadrut built up a comprehensive network of institutions to provide sickness, disability and unemployment benefits, mutual aid, pensions and a widows' fund. Members of the various settlements, the kvutzot and moshavim, for example, attained complete security in this respect, given them by the community in which they lived and to which they contributed their labor. Other groups too, labor and nonlabor, established organizations during this period to care for the health and other needs of their members. However, by enacting the present law, we are leaving the field of voluntary effort and entering a legal framework.

We are aware of the difficulties of this period in which we are about to initiate a social insurance scheme. The state is still in the process of building and consolidation, heavily burdened by defense needs, the absorption of a mass immigration, and increasing economic difficulties. When we were planning for the future and drafting this first bill, we had to take these limitations into account. These difficulties made it impossible to introduce the total plan in its entirety, and it will be implemented gradually. We also had to refrain from laying too heavy a burden on the treasury at this early stage.

National insurance, for the first few years at least, will be the means by which capital will be accumulated and money withdrawn from circulation, thus contributing to the fight against inflation. As far as insurance payments made by employers for their workers are concerned, in one specific instance—that of industrial accidents—future benefits will, in many cases, be much smaller than those paid at present by private insurance companies. In those cases where firms already have pension and insurance schemes, pensions and sums paid in cases of death will not be increased. Where benefits do increase, this will stem, above all, from the very nature of social insurance. Its integral components consist of the mutual responsibility of its members, equalization of the financial burden according to means, the spreading of risk, the responsibility of one age group for another, and the unification of management and executive.

We are not the only country that initiated a national insurance scheme at a time of great economic hardship. England did so, as have many others who regarded social insurance as an important social and economic instrument of progress.

And now to the content of the bill. I have already said that it is only the first part of a comprehensive national insurance plan. At this stage it is introducing old age pensions, widows' and orphans' benefits (called death insurance in the bill), maternity grants, and industrial accident insurance. The subsequent stages should include health, disability, and unemployment insurance.

11. The Israeli Action in Sinai: 1956

This statement was made by Mrs. Meir, then Foreign Minister of Israel, in the General Assembly of the United Nations to explain the reasons for Israel's action in the Sinai. (In English, December 5, 1956)

On the same day in May, 1948, that Egyptian bombs began to fall on Tel Aviv, the first Jewish refugee ship from the camps in Germany reached the shores of Israel. Six million of the 7,250,000 Jews of Europe, outside of the Soviet Union, had been slaughtered by the Nazis, and now the survivors were coming back not as the banned "illegals" of the mandatory regime, but to the greeting prophesied by Jeremiah: "Thy children shall come back to thy border."

These two episodes are symbolic of the life of Israel since its inception—rescue and reconstruction, menaced constantly by the destructive efforts of its neighbors.

Israel's people went forth into the desert or struck roots in stony hillsides to establish new villages, to build roads and houses and schools and hospitals; marauders, later organized as fedayeen [Arab terrorists], entering from Egypt and Jordan, were sent in to kill and destroy. Israel dug wells, brought water in pipes from great distances; Egypt sent in fedayeen to blow up the wells and the pipes.

Jews from Yemen brought in their sick, undernourished children with a tradition that two out of five would die; that number has been cut down to one out of twenty-five. While we were feeding those babies and curing their diseases, the fedayeen were sent in to throw bombs at children in synagogues and grenades into baby homes.

This parallel went on for eight long years, day in, day out, and night after night. Men, women, and children—the remnant who survived the Hitler atrocities and the more than 400,000 Jews from Arab-speaking countries, broken in body and spirit, people seeking to rebuild their lives, the new settlers of the Negev desert—these were the objects of the terror to which we were subjected.

For eight years, now, Israel has been subjected to the unremitting violence of physical assault and to an equally unremitting intent to destroy our country economically through blockade, through boycott, and through lawless interference with the development of our natural resources. Since Israel's efforts to repulse the concerted Arab onslaught in 1948, my country has had no respite from hostile acts and loudly proclaimed threats of destruction.

It would be idle to pretend that the present situation can be discussed without regard to this background or that the causes that precipitated Israel's recent security action can be ignored. If this Assembly is genuinely determined to restore peace to the Middle East, it must first determine from which source aggressive policies derive. It will serve little purpose to isolate one link in the chain of circumstances, to thrust the weight of resolutions upon one incident without considering the total effect.

Unless the United Nations is prepared to use its influence to prevail upon the countries of the Middle East to negotiate a fundamental solution, the Middle Eastern caldron will continue to seethe and the region will be a powder keg for others anxious to exploit its inflammable possibilities. Not only the well-being of Israel, but perhaps the peace of mankind, demand that the question of responsibility for unrest in this part of the world be faced and the causes of tension removed.

Israel is ringed by hostile states which invoke the terms of the 1949 Armistice Agreements when they find it convenient and which flout those agreements when they find them oppressive. They refuse to sign peace treaties, clinging desperately to the discredited theory of a "belligerent status" against Israel, while at the same time piously demanding the protections of peace for themselves. As long ago as 12 June, 1951, an official Egyptian representative defended his country's obstruction of Israeli shipping through the Suez Canal with the following extraordinary words: "We are exercising a right of war. We are still legally at war with Israel. An armistice does not put an end to a state of war. It does not prohibit a country from exercising certain rights of war."

We know from agonizing experience what these "certain rights of war" are. They include indiscriminate terror, arson, and economic attack. At the same time, any Israeli effort to stop murder and pillage, so as to make existence tolerable for its beleaguered population, is met with an outcry about the violation of peace, a peace which exists only insofar as it accords with the convenience of those who have broken it. A comfortable division has been made: The Arab states unilaterally enjoy the "rights of war"; Israel has the unilateral responsibility of keeping the peace.

But belligerency is not a one-way street. Is it surprising if a people laboring under this monstrous distinction should finally become restive and at last seek a way of rescuing its life from the perils of regulated war conducted against it from all sides?

For the people of Israel, this paradox is not merely a question of logic or semantics. Among the "rights of war" exercised against Israel has been the fedayeen campaign unleashed by Colonel Nasser in the summer of 1955. You know who these fedayeen are. They are gunmen, trained by Egyptian Army officers and recruited chiefly from among the Arab population in the Gaza Strip, which was captured by the Egyptian Army when it invaded Israel in 1948. Fedayeen gangs have been planted in Jordan, Lebanon, and Syria. Very heavy concentrations of these fedayeen units were stationed in the Sinai Desert. Israel's narrow borders and long frontiers make it particularly vulnerable to terror squads who cross the border at night with the sole objective of indiscriminately shooting or bombing any Israeli house or any man, woman, or child.

The murders committed by the fedayeen were hailed by the Cairo radio on 31 August, 1955, with words which left no doubt as to the identity of the organizers of these outrages: "Weep, O Israel, because Egypt's Arabs have already found their way to Tel Aviv. The day of extermination draws near. There shall be no more complaints or protests to the United Nations or the Armistice Commission. There will be no peace on the borders, because we demand the death of Israel."

The slaughter of six children and their teacher in the agricultural school of Shafrir, the bombing of a wedding in the Negev village of Pattish: these are examples familiar to the world of the kind of heroic exploits so lustily applauded by Colonel Nasser when he addressed a fedayeen unit in the Gaza Strip in the following terms: "You have proven by your deeds that you are heroes upon whom our entire country can depend. The spirit with which you entered the land of the enemy must be spread."

The list of daily murders, of acts of robbery and sabotage can be indefinitely extended. But let me only remind this Assembly of the events of 23 September of this year on another front, when a group of archaeologists were fired upon in Ramat Rachel from the Jordanian border. Five Israelis were killed and sixteen wounded. The next day two more Israelis—a man and a woman —working in their fields in different parts of the country, were killed by Jordanian units.

When, in response, on 25 September, deterrent action was taken at Husan by an Israel Army unit, this action was officially described by the United Nations representative as "unprovoked."

May I say that the people of Israel cannot emulate, nor do they understand, this legalistic detachment. When their peaceable fellow citizens are murdered in cold blood, in the course of their daily occupations, they are provoked, and they demand that their government reflect that sense of provocation by affording them the protection which every state owes its citizens and which international bodies are apparently unable to provide.

If moral distinctions are to be made, then let me suggest that controlled military actions—with limited and well-defined military or police objectives—are less abhorrent, even to the most sensitive conscience, than wanton and indiscriminate murder which strikes not at military targets, but solely at civilians.

The campaign of terror unleashed against Israel was not stopped by the intervention of the United Nations. The cease-fire secured by the Secretary-General last April was not honored. Instead, despite Israel's exemplary compliance with the cease-fire agreement, violence was immediately resumed and increased on every border.

Every sign pointed to the fact that the Egyptian dictator was about to realize his cherished and well-publicized ambition of a second round aimed at destroying Israel. He had amassed huge stocks of heavy armaments, secured largely from the Soviet Union and affiliated countries. He had concluded treaties with Jordan and Syria according to which the military forces of those countries were placed under the Egyptian High Command. We knew of large concentrations of armor and fedayeen in the Egyptian bases in the Sinai Desert and the Gaza Strip directly along the borders of Israel. There was a minimum of reticence about the proposed "extermination" of the small neighboring state.

We recognized the symptoms. Within the lifetime of nearly every person here present, a dictator arose, who, like this disciple of his, informed the world in advance of his bloodthirsty plans. The ashes of the crematoria, the carnage of millions, a world in ruin, testified to the fidelity with which he kept his promises. Such a lesson should not be forgotten. Certainly the people of Israel are not likely to forget what the threat of total extermination means.

It is not my intention to enter here into a description of the acts of hostility of the Egyptian government in many other fields. But the Assembly cannot remain indifferent, above all, to the fact that ever since the Security Council resolution of 1 September, 1951, was adopted—and indeed, before that—the government of Israel has patiently striven to solve the grave international problem of a double sea blockade imposed against Israel by Egypt in the Suez Canal and in the Straits of Aqaba. The Security Council confirmed the illegality of this blockade and rejected the Egyptian argument of a "state of war" by which Egypt sought to justify the blockade. The Council ordered Egypt to terminate these practices.

In October, 1956, the Security Council repeated its call for free passage without any discrimination, "overt or covert." These decisions have been flouted. At the same time Egypt and the other Arab countries have sought by every means, direct and indirect, by organized boycott and by indiscriminate threats and attempted blackmail of countries friendly to Israel, to cripple Israel's commerce and to strangle its economic life. It has extended that boycott of Israel even to the agencies of this very organization, the United Nations.

We are a very small people in a small barren land which we have revived with our labor and our love. The odds against us are heavy; the disparity of forces is great; we have, however, no alternative but to defend our lives and freedom and the right to security. We desire nothing more than peace, but we cannot equate peace merely with an apathetic readiness to be destroyed. If hostile forces gather for our proposed destruction, they must not demand that we provide them with ideal conditions for the realization of their plans. Nor should it be permitted that the sincere desire for peace, shared by so many, should be used as the shelter for such preparations.

The action of the Israel Army in the unpopulated Sinai Desert served to disrupt well-laid Egyptian plans and to liquidate new bases of active hostility against us. The texts of captured Egyptian military documents which Israel presented to the Security Council on 15 November indicate how imminent was the attack. I shall not repeat the long and detailed directives to the Egyptian commanders. But it would be salutary for all of us not to forget the introduction which read: "Every commander is to prepare himself and his subordinates for the inevitable campaign with Israel for the purpose of fulfilling our exalted aim which is the annihilation of Israel and its destruction in the shortest possible time in the most brutal and cruel battles."

I wonder if there are any other countries represented in this Assembly which live under similar conditions. And I wonder whether there is a people in the world prepared to commit itself to a policy by which, if placed in Israel's situation, it would take no action in self-defense.

Is it conceivable that this Assembly should view the situation in Israel preceding 29 October, 1956, as one of peace? Why should acts of cowardly murder of unarmed men, women, and children, carried out for years, evoke less resentment than an open military operation against nests of fedayeen and bases of hostile forces?

The practical problems which, it is claimed, divide the Arabs and Israel are not beyond solution. The world has, for instance, known and still knows refugee problems of far wider scope than that of the Arab refugees. In Korea, in India and Pakistan, in Greece and Turkey, in Europe and the Second World War, these numerically far larger problems have been or are being successfully handled. Who more than the Jewish people have endured the tragic fate of the refugee? If today there is no bitter Jewish refugee problem in the world, it is because Israel, supported by the solidarity of the Jewish people everywhere and with the aid of friendly governments, has largely solved it.

There need never have been a Palestine Arab refugee problem at all, had it not been created by the action of the Arab states. Given the cooperation of those same Arab states, this distressing human problem could readily have been solved and can be solved today. In its solution Israel, as has been previously stated on behalf of my government, is prepared to play its part.

But while Israel was absorbing Jewish refugees to a number exceeding that of all the Arab refugees—hundreds of thousands of those whom we absorbed came from those same Arab lands— the Arab states for their part, with the exception of Jordan, were erecting an iron wall between themselves and these kinsmen of theirs. And since then they have lost no opportunity of exploiting these people as a political weapon in their war against Israel.

The fundamental problem in the whole situation is the systematically organized Arab hostility against Israel. Arab enmity toward Israel is not a natural phenomenon. It is artificially fostered and nurtured. It is not, as has been here alleged, Israel which is an instrument of colonialism. It is the Israel-Arab conflict which keeps the area at the mercy of dangerously contending outside forces. Only by the liquidation of that conflict will the people of the region be able to work out their own destinies in independence and hope. Only in that prospect lies hope for a brighter future of equality and progress for all the peoples concerned. If hatred is abandoned as a principle of Arab policies, everything becomes possible.

Over and over again the Israel government has held out its hand in peace to its neighbors. But to no avail. At the ninth session of the General Assembly, the Israel representative suggested that if the Arab countries were not yet ready for peace, it would be useful, as a preliminary or transitory stage, to conclude agreements committing the parties to policies of nonaggression and pacific settlement. The reply was outright rejection. Our offer to meet the representatives of all or any of the Arab countries still stands. Never have we heard an echo from across our borders to our call for peace.

The concept of annihilating Israel is a legacy of Hitler's war against the Jewish people, and it is no mere coincidence that the soldiers of Nasser had an Arabic translation of *Mein Kampf* in their knapsacks. Those concerned sincerely with peace and freedom in the world would, I think, have been happier had some more ennobling literature been offered these men as a guide. We are convinced that these dangerous seeds have not yet succeeded in corrupting the Arab peoples. This fatal game is one which the Arab political leaders should halt in the interests of the Arab peoples themselves.

I wish at this point to renew an appeal already heard from this rostrum to Egypt to desist from the shameful and disastrous policy recently initiated of wholesale persecution of its Jewish population.

I shall not elaborate on the mass of detailed information now reaching us in this connection, some of which has been incorporated in a memorandum which it was my honor to transmit to the Assembly on 1 December—the sordid and disgraceful story of deportations and concentration camps, of indignity and spoliation, of the holding of hostages to ensure silence on the part of those expelled, and of callous brutality. I can only hope that the shocked conscience of the world will have its effect on the rulers of Egypt and that they will yet desist, and desist at once, from the measures on which they have embarked.

What ought to be done now? Are we, in our relations with Egypt, to go back to an armistice regime which has brought anything but peace and which Egypt has derisively flouted? Shall the Sinai Desert again breed nests of fedayeen and be the staging ground of aggressive armies posed for the assault? Must the tragedy again be reenacted in the tinderbox of the Middle East? The peace of our region and perhaps of more than our region hangs on the answers which will be given to these questions.

In a letter of 4 November, 1956, to the Secretary-General of the United Nations, we put the following questions:

"Does Egypt still adhere to the position declared and maintained by it over years that it is in a state of war with Israel?

"Is Egypt prepared to enter into immediate negotiations with Israel with a view to the establishment of peace between the two countries as indicated in the aide-mémoire of the Government of Israel of 4 November 1956 to the Secretary-General of the United Nations?

"Does Egypt agree to cease economic boycott against Israel and lift the boycott of Israel shipping in the Suez Canal?

"Does Egypt undertake to recall fedayeen gangs under its control in other Arab countries?"

Is it too much to expect clear, simple, binding answers? Are we, and not only we but you fellow members of the United Nations, to take as an answer the announcement on Cairo radio, on 2 December, 1956, repeated again later in the day, that: "The fedayeen command has decided to launch a fierce campaign within Israel during the coming winter season"? Can the United Nations make itself responsible for the restoration, once again on our southern borders, of murder and sabotage units pursuing a one-sided belligerency?

The blockade in the Gulf of Aqaba is now terminated. The battery of guns installed a few years ago by the Egyptian government on the desolate and empty shore at the southern tip of the Sinai Peninsula for the sole illegal purpose of preventing the passage into the gulf of Israeli shipping no longer exists. Would it not be grotesque for an international body to permit the creation anew of the conditions which made that blockade possible or to permit Egypt to perpetuate unhindered its parallel blockade in Suez? We cannot believe that this is the case. To do so would constitute a distortion of the very meaning and essence of the Charter.

My government has undertaken an obligation to withdraw its forces from Egyptian territory, and we are implementing it. But we must know—I think the Assembly must know—what will be the role of the United Nations Force after the Israeli forces are withdrawn. We are certain that it is not the intention of the Assembly to re-create the conditions laden with the identical dangers which produced the explosion of 29 October.

May I remind the representatives of the Soviet Union that there was a time, not so long ago, when they understood Israel's right to self-defense and appreciated the true disposition of forces in the Middle East? Mr. Jacob Malik declared in the Council in 1948 in words which are as apt today as the day they were uttered: "Ever since its birth this state [of Israel] declared that it wished to live in peace and entertain peaceful relations with all its neighbors. . . . It is not to blame for the fact that this appeal did not meet with any response from its neighbors."

The truth is that, since 1948, when the words of the USSR representative that I have quoted were uttered, nothing has changed in Israel's desire or intentions. We seek, as before, to fulfill our historic mission of rebuilding our land for our harried people and to live in peace with our neighbors. But I say again neither peace nor war can be unilateral. A boundary must be respected by two sides; it cannot be open to fedayeen and closed to Israeli soldiers.

What does Israel want? Its requirements are simple. We wish to be secure against threats to our territorial integrity and national independence. We wish to be left alone to pursue the work of developing our country and building a new society founded on social justice and individual liberty. We wish to cooperate with our neighbors for the common good of all the peoples of the region.

These objectives do no more than give practical expression to the principles and purpose of our Charter. These are not special claims; they are the aims and policies of all peace-loving members of the United Nations.

I would urge this Assembly to think of the future with the same vigor and insistence that it has dealt with recent events. Can this Assembly leave this subject without raising its voice, with all the authority it carries, in a call to all the governments of the region immediately to enter into direct negotiations with the purpose of arriving at a peace settlement? We, the people of Israel, believe not only in the necessity but also in the possibility of peace.

Only last Wednesday, 28 November, the representative of Egypt, speaking from this rostrum, made the following statement: "With the great majority of the peoples of the world, Egypt has been saying, and will continue to say, that all nations can and should, for their own good, moral as well as material, live together in equality, freedom and fraternity, and with modern science and its vast potentialities at the service of man, enabling him, carried by the momentum of liberty and faith, to live an infinitely more productive and honorable life."

With that statement we wholeheartedly concur. We for our part are ready to make it a practical reality. It is now for Egypt to do the same.

The countries of the Middle East are rightly listed in the category of the "underdeveloped." The standard of living, disease, the illiteracy of the masses of people, the undeveloped lands, desert, and swamp—all these cry out desperately for minds, hands, financial means, and technical ability. Can we envisage what a state of peace between Israel and its neighbors during the past eight years would have meant for all of us? Can we try to translate fighter planes into irrigation pipes and tractors for the people in these lands? Can we, in our imagination, replace gun emplacements by schools and hospitals? The many hundreds of millions of dollars spent on armaments could surely have been put to a more constructive purpose.

Substitute cooperation between Israel and its neighbors for sterile hatred and ardor for destruction, and you give life and hope and happiness to all its people.

12. Israel Withdraws from Sinai: 1957

At the United Nations General Assembly, Foreign Minister Meir announced the withdrawal of Israeli forces from Sinai, Aqaba, and Gaza. Her discussion of the problems implicit in this withdrawal are particularly relevant to the current situation in the Middle East in view of the immediate violation by Egypt of the terms accepted by Israel when it agreed to withdraw its units. (In English, January 17, 1957)

I rise to make a statement on the problems of the Sinai Desert, the Gulf of Aqaba, and the Gaza Strip.

On 3 December, 1956, Israeli forces withdrew from the Suez Canal area along the length of the Canal to a distance of some 50 kilometers. This action enabled the United Nations Emergency Force to take up its position for the first time along the Suez Canal and to create conditions in which the work of clearance might begin. The Secretary-General in his discussions with Israel representatives had indicated that the clearing of the Suez Canal was the most urgent and immediate problem, after which one could deal with the general problem of withdrawal in the Sinai Desert and finally with the particular problem of the Sharm el-Sheikh area.

Subsequent phases of withdrawal carried out during December and January followed this scheme of priorities.

On 8 January, 1957, Israeli forces withdrew to a more easterly line, leaving no Israeli forces west of El Arish. As a result of this action, the major part of the Sinai Desert was evacuated. Thus the undertaking of the Israel government transmitted by the Secretary-General to the General Assembly on 24 December had been precisely fulfilled.

On 8 January, as soon as the previous phase of withdrawal had been completed, the Israel government informed the Secretary-General of its decision to withdraw another 25 to 30 kilometers throughout the Sinai Desert except in the area of Sharm el-Sheikh. This action enabled the entry of United Nations Emergency Forces into El Arish and the St. Catherine's Monastery.

On 14 January, one day before the previous phase of withdrawal·was due for completion, the Israel government communicated its decision to have the Sinai Desert entirely evacuated by Israel forces on 22 January with the exception of the Sharm el-Sheikh area—that is, the strip on the west coast of the Gulf of Aqaba which at present ensures freedom of navigation through the Straits of Tiran and in the Gulf of Aqaba. At the same time my government informed the Secretary-General of its willingness to enter forthwith into conversations with him in connection with the evacuation of this strip. At the meeting of 14 January the Israel representative also indicated the desire of my government to begin discussions at an early date on the arrangements envisaged for the Gaza area.

From this narrative the General Assembly will observe that the withdrawals in the Sinai Desert have followed an orderly system of phasing, in coordination with the eastward movement of United Nations Emergency Forces following closely behind. By 22 January Israel will have evacuated approximately 30,000 square miles of territory which it had held at the end of November, when the United Nations Emergency Force first became capable of following up the Israeli withdrawals in force as envisaged in the General Assembly's resolution of 7 November.

It is evident, therefore, that my government cannot accept— nor can any objective mind sustain—any criticism of Israel's action in carrying out its undertaking of 8 November "to withdraw its forces from Egyptian territory as soon as satisfactory arrangements can be made with the United Nations in connection with the United Nations Emergency Force."

On the basis of the discussions which its representatives have had during this phased withdrawal, my government understands that there will not be any joint occupation in the area between Egyptian forces and UNEF forces; we believe that it should be the policy of the United Nations to maintain separation between Egyptian and Israeli forces.

Before I discuss the complex problems which now confront us, I wish to comment on the circumstances which have attended these efforts by Israel to fulfill the objectives of the General Assembly. The position can be briefly stated. Throughout these weeks during which Israel has cooperated actively with the United Nations on the withdrawal of troops, there has not been one single act of compliance by Egypt with the recommendations of policies of the international organization, to which she has looked for protection against the consequences of her own belligerency.

While the General Assembly's resolution of 2 November established special priority for an immediate cease-fire, it also contained other recommendations, not one of which the Egyptian government has shown any intention to fulfill.

The 2 November resolution urged that "upon the cease-fire being effective, steps be taken to reopen the Suez Canal and restore secure freedom of navigation." This objective, so vital for the security and economic welfare of many countries, has been subjected by Egypt to every kind of obstruction and delay; conditions and provisos have been attached to every phase of its implementation. No action has been spared which might slow the process down; steps essential for the clearance of the Canal have been made conditional on the policies and preferences of the territorial power. Negotiations aiming at establishing international law in the operation of the Suez Canal have been delayed, at Egypt's behest. Above all, the Egyptian government has given no indication that when the Canal is open, it will not again be exposed to the illegality and discrimination which Egypt has maintained for the past six years, in defiance of a decision by the Security Council.

A similar fate has befallen the injunction of the General Assembly in its 2 November resolution "to desist from raids across the armistice lines in the neighboring territory." Fedayeen gangs, operating in neighboring countries under Egyptian direction, continue to spread death and havoc throughout our countryside. Since 3 December when the Cairo radio announced the intention of the Nasser regime to conduct raids into Israel throughout the winter, some thirty assaults have been committed. The official media of information in Egypt have reported these attacks in boastful communiqués. It is evident that in this respect, too, Egypt claims the fulfillment of Assembly resolutions by others, without any parallel acts of compliance on her part.

Moreover, during a period in which the United Nations has used its full influence on Egypt's behalf for the withdrawal of troops, Egyptian policy has been marked by a grave violation of Charter principles and of fundamental human rights. Foreign nationals have been expropriated and deported. The Jewish community has been subjected to a persecution recalling some of the excesses of totalitarianism before and during the Second World War. Seven thousand Egyptian Jews have been driven out by this organized cruelty, and all the conditions for a panic-stricken exodus have been willfully created by the Nasser regime. Thousands of victims have reached Israel's welcoming shores. Some member governments, in their direct relationships with Egypt, have been moved to express mounting indignation and concern.

World opinion has been quick to perceive the disparity between the assistance which Egypt has received of the United Nations and the complete absence of any Egyptian response to the legitimate interests of other states and of the organized international community. The question whether Israel is not withdrawing into a position of exposure to renewed Egyptian bel ligerency, by land and sea, arises in our mind with increasing anxiety and concern.

The acuteness of this question will be easily perceived if we recall that twelve weeks have elapsed since my government addressed four questions to the Egyptian government which have still not been answered:

1. Does Egypt still adhere to the position declared and maintained by her over years that she is in a state of war with Israel?
2. Is Egypt prepared to enter into immediate negotiations with Israel with a view to the establishment of peace between the two countries as indicated in paragraph 3 of the aide-mémoire of the government of Israel of 4 November, 1956, to the Secretary-General of the United Nations?
3. Does Egypt agree to cease economic boycott against Israel and lift the blockade of Israel shipping in the Suez Canal?
4. Does Egypt undertake to recall fedayeen gangs under her control in other Arab countries?

In our talks with the Secretary-General on withdrawal it was mutually understood at all times that the Sharm el-Sheikh and Gaza areas were reserved for discussions at a later stage in the withdrawal process. Thus, if the reservation of these problems to this later stage were now made a source of criticism or blame, a serious injustice would be incurred, to the grave prejudice of future discussions. These problems are of special complexity; they touch the question of Israel's security at its most sensitive point. They cannot be treated lightly, without danger to international peace and security. In each case, a change in the existing situation without simultaneous measures to prevent the renewal of belligerency would lead to a possibility—nay, even a certainty—of tension and hostility.

I now come to explain why these problems have this special character and why we must all work with care and precision at the stage which we have now reached in our deliberations.

THE STRAITS OF TIRAN

The strip of territory in the Sharm el-Sheikh area commands the entrance to the Gulf of Aqaba through the Straits of Tiran. The only channel leading from the Red Sea to the gulf passes between the island of Tiran and the southeast extremity of the Sinai coast.

This channel is 3 miles in width, but its navigable part is only some 500 meters broad. Thus any ship passing to or from the Gulf of Aqaba must come very close to the Sinai coast.

At a point in the Sharm el-Sheikh area known as Ras Nasrani, Egypt set up gun emplacements six years ago for the sole purpose of preventing ships from sailing freely in the Gulf of Aqaba to and from the port of Elath. Two of these were 6-inch guns and four 3-inch guns. They were trained on the only lane usable by ships as they sail through the straits. These guns have blockaded the Gulf of Aqaba for the past six years.

Sharm el-Sheikh, Ras Nasrani, and the neighboring islands are uninhabited, waterless and desolate. The only purpose of any human presence in these places until 3 November was to prevent free access to an international waterway. The purpose of our presence since then has been to ensure free access. It is astonishing to observe the elaborate installations, the ammunition depots, the airstrip, the spacious accommodations which the Egyptians had established, with the sole aim of obstructing the free passage of commerce between two parts of the high seas.

These installations were established towards the end of 1949. In reply to a query addressed to it by the American embassy in Cairo, the Egyptian government, on 28 January, 1950, gave assurances that it had no intention of interfering with peaceful shipping and that passage through the straits would "as in the past remain free in conformity with international practice and with recognized principles of international law." This Egyptian document has been recorded in full in the verbatim records of the Security Council.

In spite of this assurance and of the fact that the Gulf of

Aqaba is a recognized waterway, Egypt has used its gun emplacements to blockade the passage of ships bound for Elath through the Straits of Tiran. The blockade in the Suez Canal, which was condemned by the Security Council in 1951, has been carried out by Egypt with equal stringency—and illegality—in the Gulf of Aqaba.

The blockade works primarily through its deterrent effect, but many acts of force have been committed against ships exercising innocent passage in this international waterway. Fire has been opened on British, American, and Italian ships; interference and obstruction have been offered to vessels of Norwegian, Danish, and other flags. These acts of piracy had almost eliminated commerce and navigation in the Gulf of Aqaba, slowed down the development of the port of Elath, inflicted illicit injury on Israel's economy and trade, and denied other countries an alternative route to the Suez Canal, as a link between the Red Sea and the Mediterranean.

On 3 November, when Israel forces entered the Sharm el-Sheikh area to assure Israel's self-defense against wanton belligerency, these guns were silenced. Today, for the first time, ships of all nations are free to move north and south through the Straits of Tiran to and from Elath. An alternative link to Suez joining the Red Sea and Mediterranean is now open to all shipping without distinction of flag.

In his Note to the General Assembly the Secretary-General refers to "the international significance of the Gulf of Aqaba" which justifies "the right of innocent passage through the Straits of Tiran and the Gulf in accordance with rules of international law." In 1949 the International Court of Justice ruled that when straits are geographically part of a highway used for international navigation, the vessels of all nations enjoy the right of free passage therein, whether or not the straits are entirely or partly within the territorial waters of one or more states. In the words of the court, they belong to the class of international highways through which passage cannot be prohibited by a coastal state.

The international character of the Gulf of Aqaba and the

Straits of Tiran is fully confirmed by the jurisprudence of the United Nations. In 1951, the Security Council denounced the Egyptian blockade against Israel, as inconsistent with Egypt's international obligations. In particular, the Security Council denied Egypt the right to exercise visit, search, or seizure or to apply restrictions against shipping on the grounds of "belligerent rights." Egypt was called upon to cease all such practices. While the Council's decision was prompted by the Egyptian illegalities in the Suez Canal, its judgments against visit, search, or seizure are couched in broader terms, so as to be of general application.

In March, 1954, the Security Council discussed an Israeli complaint against Egyptian restrictions both in the Suez Canal and the Gulf of Aqaba. The majority voted for a resolution condemning these restrictions, wherever applied, and calling for their immediate cessation. This resolution was presented by New Zealand and supported by the United States, the United Kingdom, France, Brazil, Colombia, Turkey, and Denmark. Interpreting the majority view, the New Zealand representative said: "The final paragraph of the draft resolution (para. 6) refers only to the complaint of interference with ships in the Gulf of Aqaba. . . . The arguments advanced by the representatives of Egypt in justification of that interference cannot be sustained and in fact have already been rejected by the Council."

Thus the illegal character of Egypt's restrictions is established by recognized principles of international law, by the jurisprudence of the Security Council and of the International Court of Justice, by the consensus of the maritime powers, and even by Egypt's own admission in its assurance to the United States on 28 January, 1950.

Israel is the only country in the world, except Egypt, with a coastline both on the Mediterranean and on the Red Sea. The fact that its territory unites the eastern and western oceans across a land bridge of less than 150 miles constitutes Israel's most important geographical advantage; to have had this facility denied by illegal action for many years is an outrage which should no longer be suffered. Indeed, having in recent weeks experienced the use of this open international waterway, Israel can surely not be asked to acquiesce in its ever being closed again. The development of the southern part of our country; the expansion of our port facilities at Elath; our right of free commerce with friendly nations in Africa and Asia; the vision of our country as a bridge between the traffic and ideas of the Eastern and Western worlds; the liberation of countries in Europe and Asia from exclusive dependence on a single Canal at Suez, exploited by Egypt to hold other states up to injury and extortion; the consequent denial to Egypt of a position of monopoly and domination, unhealthy both for itself and for the maritime nations—all these great issues are bound up in the problem of ensuring free passage through the Gulf of Aqaba and the Straits of Tiran. The more this problem is contemplated, the bigger it becomes. It is an issue of broad international scope.

Israel is not alone in having a vital interest in the permanent maintenance of free navigation in the Gulf of Aqaba. Countries whose economy depends upon the flow of trade between the Red Sea and the Mediterranean have already suffered loss through the Egyptian blockade in this international waterway. The gulf, freed from the illegal Egyptian blockade, can become a pivotal point of international commerce. The port facilities at Elath are being constantly improved. Communications of all kinds across the relatively short land link between the two seas are under active improvement, and other projects are in a planning stage. If this position is not impaired, then no single state, and therefore no state at all, will have a stranglehold on the jugular vein of other nations.

The relevance of this consideration is already shown by an item appearing in this morning's New York *Times*.

The avoidance of any renewed blockade in the Gulf of Aqaba and the Straits of Tiran is an objective which the government of Israel is resolved to pursue with the utmost tenacity. We have no national interests superior to this. We cannot take the responsibility of allowing this interest to be endangered and of seeing Egyptian guns ever again set up to obstruct the commerce of nations in this international waterway.

Nor, I believe, will the United Nations wish to assume that responsibility. It is unthinkable that our organization should, for whatever motive, be instrumental in restoring an illicit blockade. What would history say of the United Nations which for the past five years has not been able to keep the Suez Canal open without discrimination, if it should now be instrumental in obstructing the alternative route between the Red Sea and the Mediterranean? Is it not sufficient that Egypt's policies have denied the world the use of the Suez Canal? Must the blockade also be brought back to the only alternative route? For nine years Egypt has refused to maintain a legal situation in the Suez Canal. Is it conceivable that similar discrimination should be brought back to the Gulf of Aqaba and the Straits of Tiran?

But this result, shocking as it seems, would certainly occur if the United Nations were to press for Israel's withdrawal, without, at the same time, establishing effective arrangements for ensuring permanent freedom of navigation through the straits and the gulf. Unless special measures are now instituted, Israel's withdrawal, after an uncertain interlude of United Nations Emergency Force occupation, would be succeeded by the establishment of Egyptian guns. The open waterway would again become a closed lake. Ships would be detained and assaulted. Since Israel can never again allow her legitimate commerce to be intercepted in the Gulf, Egyptian belligerency would have dire effects. That this prospect is very real is proved by an Egyptian broadcast a few days ago: "The Arabs will pursue every Israeli ship which tries to pass into the Gulf of Aqaba until they destroy her." In August, 1951, in discussing Egypt's maritime blockade, the representative of Brazil uttered a grave warning. He said: "Should we accept the Egyptian thesis, we would be bound to recognize any measures of reprisal adopted by the Israel government. It is obvious that in the exchange of hostile acts that would follow we could hardly expect to lay the foundations of a definite solution to the Palestine question." Thus, the establishment of effective guarantees for permanent freedom of navigation in the gulf and the straits is essential not only for the defense of international and Israeli interests, but also for the preservation of peace. If conflict were to break out, who can be sure to what it might lead?

Because the problem of the Sharm el-Sheikh area raises such grave issues, it has been reserved for discussion to this late stage. It was no doubt for this reason that in conversations between the Israeli delegate and the Secretary-General it was mutually understood that the very complication of the problems and the international interest involved implied a need for negotiation in order to safeguard that international interest and that therefore this belonged to a later stage of the general withdrawal.

Surely no delegate who studies this problem can doubt its gravity. Our sole aim and interest in the Sharm el-Sheikh area is to ensure that we take no action now which would leave even the smallest chance of such a tragic result as the restoration of the blockade and the consequent renewal of regional conflict and of international tension.

On the other hand, a solution is not impossible. My delegation has variant proposals in mind which it will be prepared to explore in the continuing course of its discussions on the problems of withdrawal. Ways can be sought of simultaneously reconciling two objectives—the withdrawal of Israeli forces and the effective guaranteeing of permanent freedom of navigation in this international waterway.

The mere entry into this area of United Nations Emergency Force, even with the specific aim of preventing belligerency, would not in itself be a solution. For there is yet no clarity about the functions of the United Nations Emergency Force or about the duration of its tenure. Any temporary measure for preventing belligerency and securing free navigation would not be effective unless it were ensured in advance that it would operate until a peace settlement were achieved or until some other effective measure were established by international guarantees for ensuring permanent freedom of navigation. Such guarantees could, perhaps, be furnished either by the principal maritime powers, or by an agreement between the four coastal states, or by some combination of the two forms of guarantee. But, if the United Nations Emergency Force were to be regarded as a key to the solution of this problem, greater clarity and precision would be needed in defining its functions and the conditions and duration of its tenure.

THE GAZA STRIP

In his Note to the General Assembly the Secretary-General states that "further discussions with the representatives of Israel are required" on the question of the Gaza Strip. On 14 January, Israel representatives stated that they were ready for such discussions at an early date. At this stage I wish only to describe the general background of our thinking on the Gaza question.

When the state of Israel was established in 1948, the Egyptian Army crossed the Sinai Desert into the Negev, in defiance of the cease-fire resolution of the Security Council, in an attempt to destroy Israel's newborn independence by force of arms. The attack was held by the Israeli settlements in the Negev. The Egyptians were driven back across the international frontier into Sinai. They succeeded, however, in clinging to a narrow rectangular strip 6 miles wide extending north from the Egyptian frontier for 26 miles along the Mediterranean coast to a point within 35 miles of Tel Aviv.

In the summer of 1955 the Nasser regime launched a new form of aggression against Israel from the Gaza Strip. Amongst the destitute elements of the local population and refugee camps, the Egyptian High Command organized fedayeen units as military formations of the Egyptian Army. In the past eighteen months, these units carried out an intensified campaign of attack upon Israel. They ambushed road traffic, killed men, women, and children, blew up wells and water installations, mined roads at night, demolished houses in which farmers and their families were peacefully asleep. These outrages culminated in major outbreaks during August and September, 1955, April, 1956 and October, 1956.

In the ominous buildup of Egyptian forces, with offensive

weapons obtained during the first half of 1956, the Gaza Strip had an essential role both as a center for fedayeen groups and as the forward base of an Egyptian Army division which was stationed there within an hour's drive from Tel Aviv.

Since the expulsion of Egyptian forces from Gaza, fedayeen have ceased to infest the countryside. When the tensions and hostilities had died down in early November, the refugee camps became calm. Israeli farmers and their families in the Negev had at last attained physical security. Since 3 November no house, no school, no baby home in their villages has been shelled from across the border.

The report submitted by the representative of the Secretary-General, Colonel Nelson, who visited the Gaza Strip at the end of November, lies before the General Assembly as Document A/3491. According to this report, "the Israel authorities have methodically established a program to stabilize life in Gaza." "They have established law and order." "The execution of civic responsibilities is being worked out progressively with the local officials." "The Israel Administration allows the United Nations Relief and Works Agency complete freedom throughout the area." "A plan to make available basic foodstuffs at subsidized prices from Israel government stocks to the local non-refugee population is being worked out." "Measures were being introduced to facilitate the marketing of agricultural produce, citrus, and dates for export from the Gaza area. In speaking to several farmers there was evidence that arrangements were being made through the Israeli Citrus Board to actually export the agricultural produce."

Colonel Nelson reports on the opening of banks and credit facilities. He certifies that "there was relatively small physical damage caused in the area due to the events of the second and third of November." "On 25 November, the Israel civilian police reporting to Israel Central Police Headquarters was established in the area and is being coordinated with the local police. Throughout the area one could see both Israeli civil police and the local police patrolling." On the other hand, "there were few troops evident in the area as compared to the concentration of Egyptian troop units prior to 2 November."

Colonel Nelson goes on to report that "water installations are functioning throughout the area," that "power stations in the area are back to normal," that "telephone communication is being restored progressively," that "requisitioned cars and trucks are being progressively returned to their owners," that "hospitals are in full operation," that "Israel Health Ministry representatives have been in the area to coordinate and assist."

Religious institutions in the area are pursuing their activities without interruption. In a letter addressed on 18 November to the Israel Ministry of Religious Affairs, Monseigneur Antonio Vergani, Vicar-General in Israel of the Latin Patriarchate, stated: "I have found that everything has gone for the best and that as soon as the occupation of the town by Israel forces had started, an officer came immediately to the Latin Church, where some 1,500 persons sought refuge, and, having ascertained that no harm occurred, posted another officer and guard."

Similar tributes to a growing stability and peace in the Gaza area have been recorded by the Senior Vicar of the Armenian Patriarchate and by the representatives of the International Red Cross Committee.

The future status of the Gaza Strip remains to be determined. It must be recalled that Gaza is separated from Egypt by scores of miles of desert. The Egyptian military regime during the past eight years was provisional in character and of undefined legal status, and it resulted in the decay of the area and in the impoverishment of its population. No contribution whatever had been made by Egypt to the solution of any part of the refugee problem, despite the fact that this problem had been created through the invasion of Israel by Egypt and other Arab states in 1948. It is inconceivable to my government that the nightmare of the previous eight years should be reestablished in Gaza with international sanction. Shall Egypt be allowed once more to organize murder and sabotage in this strip? Shall Egypt be allowed to condemn the local population to permanent impoverishment and to block any solution of the refugee problem?

My government believes that a solution of Gaza's problems and especially of the problem of Arab refugees can be found. On the other hand, it must be admitted that any international force would be powerless to prevent the return of elements which would incite and intimidate the local population and the refugees and the recrudescence of fedayeen activities. Nor is it possible to maintain an area such as the Gaza Strip almost entirely devoid of economic resources in a state of economic isolation from any adjoining territory.

It will be seen that the issues which arise are complex and offer no easy solution. There are difficult political and security problems in which 80,000 residents and some 200,000 refugees are involved. It is clear that some time is needed to work out a permanent solution of all these problems. They cannot be solved overnight. The government of Israel is prepared immediately to enter into discussions in a quest for a solution. But we must not ignore the report of the representative of the Secretary-General who writes that "the removal of any effective authority from the area would cause an eruption either by the refugees or the local inhabitants in the form of looting or destruction of property." It is not difficult to envisage what suffering and dislocation would come upon this sorely tried region, if there were to be an uprooting of all those elements of social, economic, and municipal stability which have now been established. Opportunities must be nourished for bringing about radical improvement in the economic and social condition of the inhabitants and for working out a solution of the refugee problem. We believe that all this can be guaranteed by the continuance of the present administrative processes, working in cooperation with representatives of the local population and of the United Nations Relief and Works Agency and in suitable contact and relationship with the United Nations. While we are not yet ready with final proposals, we hope shortly to present detailed plans to the international community whereby the Gaza Strip would achieve peace and stability, whereby the economic future of the population will be assured, and whereby the United Nations with Israel's fullest cooperation, will be enabled to proceed effectively towards a solution of the refugee problem. The withdrawal of Israeli military forces from the Gaza Strip can well be one of the elements in the arrangements which we envisage.

We are ready at an early date to pursue our thinking along these lines with the Secretary-General in accordance with Paragraph 9 of his Note to the General Assembly. In this case, as in that of the entrance to the Gulf of Aqaba, the desire to proceed speedily with the fulfillment of the General Assembly's objectives on the withdrawal of troops should be tempered by a prudent concern for the avoidance of disruptions and dislocations and, above all, for the prevention of any risk of resuming the deadly conditions of belligerency which made Gaza a focus of international conflict during the previous eight years.

Mr. President, the General Assembly will surely have no difficulty in concluding that the problem of the Gulf of Aqaba with its broad international perspectives and the question of the Gaza Strip, with its almost unparalleled complexity, require further clarification in a cooperative spirit. I do not doubt that if the General Assembly leaves room for that consideration, the progress already recorded in the Secretary-General's note can be crowned by arrangements which will eliminate the prospect of the renewal of belligerency by land and by sea. In the pursuit of such arrangements my delegation will bend every resource of heart and mind in the days that lie ahead.

13. "A Solemn Appeal to the Arabs"

At the conclusion of a formal statement in the General Assembly Mrs. Meir abandoned her prepared text and surprised her listeners by making this spontaneous appeal to the Arabs. (In English, October 7, 1957)

From the rostrum I should like to address a solemn appeal to the Arab states of the Middle East: Israel is approaching her tenth anniversary. You did not want it to be born. You fought against the decision in the United Nations. You then attacked us by military force. We have all been witnesses to sorrow, destruction, and the spilling of blood and tears. Yet Israel is here, growing, developing, progressing. It has gained many friends, and their number is steadily increasing. We are an old tenacious people and, as our history has proved, not easily destroyed. Like you, the Arab countries, we have regained our national independence, and as with you, so with us, nothing will cause us to give it up. We are here to stay. History has decreed that the Middle East consists of an independent Israel and independent Arab states. This verdict will never be reversed.

In the light of these facts, what is the use or realism or the justice of policies and attitudes based on the fiction that Israel is not here or will somehow disappear? Would it not be better for all to build a future for the Middle East based on cooperation? Israel will exist and progress even without peace, but surely a future of peace would be better both for Israel and for her neighbors. The Arab world with its ten sovereignties and 3,000,000 square miles can well afford to accommodate itself to peaceful cooperation with Israel. Does hate for Israel and the aspiration for its destruction make one child in your country happier? Does it convert one hovel into a house? Does culture thrive on the soil of hatred? We have not the slightest doubt that eventually there will be peace and cooperation between us. This is a historic necessity for both peoples. We are prepared; we are anxious to bring it about now.

I should like to address myself to all delegates in this Assembly and especially to the powers directly involved in the problems of the Middle East. The deserts of the Middle East are in need of water, not bombers. The tens of millions of its inhabitants are craving for the means to live and not for the implements of death. I ask all of you—old members of the United Nations and the new—use your influence not to deepen the abyss of misunderstanding, but to bridge it.

And I wish to conclude with a word of deepest appreciation to those countries, member states of the United Nations, who just ten years ago helped to lay the foundations for Israel's statehood and whose continued understanding, assistance, and friendship have enabled us to weather the storms which have beset our path.

Many of these are countries without direct interest of any kind in our area. But their appreciation of the moral, the social, the historic and religious factors involved led them to profoundly held convictions which they have maintained with staunchness and with courage. Their friendship and their help will never be forgotten by the people of Israel and the Jewish people as a whole. It is a satisfaction and a joy too that with many among the new countries that have in the meantime joined the United Nations we are linked in bonds of friendship, of understanding, and of mutual aid.

In celebrating the tenth anniversary of Israel's independence we look back on a decade of struggle, of achievement in some areas, of failure in others. But by and large it has justified a thousandfold the vision of those who saw in the reestablishment of Israel's nationhood a historic act of reparation and of statesmanship. Our greatest grief has been the lack of progress toward peace with our Arab neighbors. It is our profoundest hope that the coming period may make a decisive forward step in this regard, to the inestimable benefit of all the people of the Middle East and perhaps of the entire world.

14. The Path for Developing Countries

A discussion of the problems of emerging countries given at the General Assembly. (In English, October 10, 1960)

With the admission of sixteen new members we all feel that we are in the presence of a revolutionary moment in human history. These countries represent millions of people who are now, for the first time, experiencing sovereignty and freedom in the modern world. Nothing is so debasing as national dependence and inequality, and nothing is so exhilarating as national independence and equality. No nation has been ordained to rule over others or has been fated to be ruled by others. And I maintain that even the best foreign rule cannot take the place of self-rule. It is because these basic truths are today universally accepted that the new countries were welcomed in our midst with such genuine joy.

But may I suggest that there are two dangers that face those of us who have emerged as newly independent states: first, lingering in the past and, second, the illusion that political independence will provide automatic solutions for all problems.

What do I mean by lingering in the past? It is natural that many new peoples should have unhappy and, in some cases, bitter memories. It is understandable that many of them should feel a sense of grievance against their former rulers and should view their present plight as the legacy of the past. It is to them a painful paradox that while some countries have problems of surpluses and overproduction, they should have been left behind in poverty. As they look about them at their lands, rich with minerals and vegetation—gold and diamonds, bauxite, iron and copper, cocoa and cotton, sugar and rubber—they must come to the conclusion that it was not God's will that they should be hungry.

How can we expect Africans to be impressed by the feats of the space age, when so many of their own people still are illiterate? You cannot expect a mother in an African village to be elated over the advance of medicine in the world when she sees her children suffering from trachoma, tuberculosis, and malaria. All this must be understood. It is natural that their former suffering and degradation should be remembered by these new free peoples. No people can build its future if it does not remember its past. But a people cannot live only by brooding over the past; it must invest all its energy and ability in the future.

I speak on behalf of an ancient people whose past for thousands of years has been full of tragedy, racial discrimination, and humiliation. It has been engaged in a continuous struggle to preserve its identity and its very survival—a struggle reaching its climax in our lifetime, in the Nazi design to reach a "final solution to the Jewish problem" by genocide—that is, by the extermination of a whole people. Not for one moment do we intend to forget that. Nor have we forgotten that our struggle for our rights in Palestine, under what became in effect a colonial regime, often took on tragic aspects. Yet, when we today survey our modest achievements, after thirteen years of statehood, we know that they were attained not by grieving; with our memories of the past intact, we bent all our energies on the building of the future.

This leads me to the second of the dangers which I have mentioned and which I am sure is apparent to all our friends sitting here for the first time. How well we all know that independence is not only a culmination of ardent dreams and aspirations. It is not only a victory after a long and heartbreaking struggle. It is all that, but it is also an overwhelming challenge with innumerable problems and dangers to be faced.

We, the new countries, have gained our independence in an era of man's greatest achievements. In parts of the world the standard of living and development has reached fantastic heights. We should not be told to go slow in our development; we should not be told that the advances of the developed countries have taken generations and centuries to attain. We cannot wait. We must develop quickly. As a friend from Kenya who visited Israel said: "Must I walk in an age of jet planes just because those that now have jets were walking generations ago?"

This challenge is one not only for the new nations, but for the entire world. Much has been said and done about what I would call "first aid": the sharing of food; the transfer of surplus to the hungry. But I wish to say that we will never be really free as long as our children need to be fed by others. Our freedom will be complete only when we have learned to bring forth the food that we need from our own soil. The cry that goes out from the African and Asian continents today is: Share with us not only food, but also your knowledge of how to produce it. The most frightening inequality in the world today lies in the gap between those that literally reach for the moon and those who do not know how to reach efficiently into their own soil to produce their daily necessities.

To satisfy the hunger of the mind is no less urgent than to satisfy the hunger for bread. The question is how the world can organize itself to span the time lag of generations and share this knowledge with those who need it. The science and technology of our century that have been available to the industrially advanced states must be made available freely and fully to the new nations toward the solution of their acute economic, social, and health problems.

The United Nations and its specialized agencies are devoting ever more attention to these crucial problems. In particular, through the twin instruments the Expanded Program of Technical Assistance and the Special Fund, skills and know-how are being freely shared among nations at different stages of economic progress, and latent resources are being surveyed and readied for development. The overall scope of these activities is more than double today what it was barely three years ago, but the articulate need for such assistance has grown even faster. The urgent demands of the newly independent nations in particular make it imperative to increase the resources at the disposal of the United Nations for this purpose. From our own experience we know the beneficial results of United Nations assistance, and within the limits of our possibilities, we are willing to increase our active participation in this great venture of international cooperation.

In an effort to help build a bridge between the two worlds—that of scientific progress and that of national liberation—an International Conference on Science in the Advancement of New States was convened by the Weizmann Institute of Science and the Israel Ministry of Education at Rehovoth, Israel, a few weeks ago. By the circumstances of her history, Israel feels a sense of kinship with each of these two worlds. We are a part, however modest, of the contemporary scientific and technological movement. At the same time we are one of the thirty-five nations which achieved their sovereignty since the United Nations was founded, and with most of those new nations we enjoy relations of friendship and mutual respect. The object of the Rehovoth Conference, as defined by its sponsors more than a year ago, was to "explore the capacity of science and technology to advance the life of nations which have not yet reached a momentum of development."

Those were the circumstances in which for two remarkable weeks Israel played host to an international gathering of unique composition. On the one hand, we had in our midst leading Cabinet ministers, university presidents, technicians and high government officials of many states, especially from Asia and Africa, whose chief problem is that of supplementing constitutional freedom by swifter economic and social progress. On the other hand, we welcomed eminent scientists whose achievements have transformed the pattern and prospect of life upon earth. These two groups of men—the statesmen of developing nations and the leaders of modern science—strove hard to come together in a genuine communion of mind and spirit.

Forty nations were represented at the conference—more than half of them from Asia and Africa. Also in attendance were representatives and observers from United Nations agencies and from foundations concerned with development and education in new societies. The conference adopted the Rehovoth Declaration, which recommended that:

(a) The governments of developing states should regard the furtherance of science and technology as a major objective of their national policies and make appropriate provision for funds and opportunities to achieve this end.

(b) In the secondary and higher educational systems of new and developing states, accelerated programs should be undertaken with a view to establishing a body of scientific workers and technical experts. . . .

(d) Until such time as their own scientific manpower is adequate, new and developing states would be well advised to seek the help of scientific advisers and experts from friendly countries and international agencies to help them develop a scientific practice and tradition. . . .

The conference appealed to the more advanced countries to extend such aid.

Now, while it is true that science and technology can provide the keys of knowledge, a major part of the capital needs for development must still be provided from outside sources. The International Bank for Reconstruction and Development and other international agencies are making splendid efforts to meet these needs, but the resources at their command are insufficient to win the race against population pressures. What is required is an initial injection of development capital on so massive a scale that it can put into motion self-perpetuating local forces of economic growth. It is ironic that at present the most spectacular expansion and the most rapid rise in the standards of life are taking place not in the backward but in the advanced countries—and the gap is widening every day instead of narrowing. No trickle of new capital can arrest this growing imbalance and promote a better equilibrium. I would merely mention that in the last five years production in the United States has increased 25 percent, and, what is more startling, in Western Europe it has increased 48 percent in this period, thus making that area a major economic force in the world.

The governor of the Bank of Israel, in a recent address at the Conference of the Board of Governors of the International Bank for Reconstruction and Development, pointed out that if 2 percent of the annual gross product of the industrialized nations that are members of the bank could be diverted into building up the underdeveloped nations, this would represent an amount of $17,000,000 a year—an amount which would impart a real momentum to the forward march of the underdeveloped countries. One should add to this a similar contribution on the part of the vast and rapidly increasing national product of the Soviet Union and other industrialized countries outside the bank. This, together with the possible savings of the developing countries themselves, could no doubt completely transform the present situation and ensure in a not too distant future a happier life of ever-growing opportunity for men everywhere on our earth.

This may sound extravagant, until we translate it into terms of human welfare for the greater part of mankind. That welfare cannot be achieved by congratulatory speeches on Independence Day, but only through a dramatic, pooled effort by the leading industrial countries.

15. The Trial of Eichmann

Adolf Eichmann, a key figure in the Nazi extermination program of the Jews and head of the Gestapo's Jewish Department, was tracked down by Israeli volunteers in his hiding place in Argentina and brought to stand trial in Israel. In this statement at the Security Council, Mrs. Meir answers the charge of illegality brought by the Argentine government. (In English, June 22, 1960)

I wish to say that we recognize that the persons who took Eichmann from Argentina to Israel broke the laws of Argentina. For this the Israel government has apologized to the Argentine government in its note dated 3 June, 1960, stating:

If the volunteer group violated Argentine law or interfered with matters within the sovereignty of Argentina, the government of Israel wishes to express its regret. The government of Israel requests that the special significance of bringing to trial the man responsible for the murder of millions of persons belonging to the Jewish people be taken into account and asks that due weight be given to the fact that the volunteers, who were themselves survivors of that massacre, placed this historic mission above all other considerations.

The government of Israel is fully confident that the Argentine government will show understanding of these historical and ethical factors.

But my government sincerely believes that this isolated violation of Argentine law must be seen in the light of the exceptional and unique character of the crimes attributed to Eichmann, on the one hand, and the motives of those that acted in this unusual manner, on the other hand. These men belong, as I do, to a people whose tragedy in the Second World War is unmatched in history. No people in modern times has ever mourned the loss of one third of its people in so short a period. We were 18,000,000 at the beginning of the war; we were 12,000,000 when the war was over. Six million of European Jewry were gassed and murdered, and among them over 1,000,000 children.

Historians of this period tell us that the Nazis were responsible for the death of 12,000,000 civilians, not as a result of military operations but as a result of the naked design to enslave and annihilate those populations who did not fit into their picture of a new world order. Half of these were Jews and the other half Slavs, predominantly Russians and Poles.

Hitler divided the peoples of the world into several categories: Germans—the *Herrenvolk;* French, British, Scandinavians and a few other nations to be absorbed into the Nazi *Herrenvolk;* Slavic peoples—some to be exterminated and the rest to be turned into slaves of the Germans; Negroes were not even to be considered human; and for Jews—physical extermination of every man, woman and child. Only for Jews was there to be an immediate "final solution."

The International Military Tribunal in Nürnberg made a finding that:

> In the summer of 1941 . . . plans were made for the "final solution" of the Jewish question in all of Europe. This "final solution" meant the extermination of the Jews, which early in 1939 Hitler had threatened would be one of the consequences of an outbreak of war, and a special section in the Gestapo

under Adolf Eichmann, as head of Section B 4 of the Gestapo, was formed to carry out the policy.

In the record of the Nürnberg trial, we read what Dieter Wisliceny, Eichmann's aide, said on the process of the final solution:

> Until 1940 the general policy within the section was to settle the Jewish question in Germany and in areas occupied by Germany by means of a planned emigration. The second phase, after that date, was the concentration of all Jews, in Poland and in other territories occupied by Germany in the East, in ghettos. This period lasted approximately until the beginning of 1942. The third period was the so-called "final solution" of the Jewish question, that is, the planned extermination and destruction of the Jewish race; this period lasted until October, 1944, when Himmler gave the order to stop their destruction.

Further, in answer to a question whether in his official connection with Section IV A 4 he learned of any order which directed the annihilation of all Jews, he said: "Yes, I learned of such an order for the first time from Eichmann in the summer of 1942."

Hitler did not solve the Jewish question according to his plans. But he did annihilate 6,000,000 Jews—Jews of Germany, France, Belgium, Holland, Luxembourg, Poland, the USSR, Hungary, Yugoslavia, Greece, Italy, Czechoslovakia, Austria, Rumania, Bulgaria. With these Jews there were destroyed over 30,000 Jewish communities which for centuries had been the center of Jewish faith, learning, and scholarship. From this Jewry stemmed some of the giants in the field of arts, literature, and science. Was it only this generation of Jews of Europe that was gassed? One million children—the future generation —were annihilated. Who can encompass this picture in all its horror and its consequences for the Jewish people for many generations to come and for Israel? Here was destroyed the natural reservoir for all that is needed for a new country— learning, skill, devotion, idealism, a pioneering spirit.

And what about those who remained alive? Who are they? Each individual is a splinter of a family destroyed—each one lives in the nightmare recollection of his dearest and closest led to the crematorium. Mothers who have seen their babies thrown into the air and used as targets for Nazi bullets. Thousands upon thousands of Jewish women will never be mothers because of Nazi "scientific experiments" performed on them. Israel alone has within its borders tens of thousands of the maimed and sick, all victims of the Nazi attempt "to solve the Jewish question."

Rudolf Hoess, the commandant of Auschwitz concentration camp, testified at the Nürnberg trial as follows:

> We had two SS doctors on duty at Auschwitz to examine the incoming transports of prisoners. The prisoners would be marched by one of the doctors, who would make spot decisions as they walked by. Those who were fit for work were sent into the camp. Others were sent immediately to the extermination plants. Children of tender years were invariably exterminated since by reason of their youth they were unable to work. . . . Very frequently women would hide their children under their clothes but, of course, when we found them we would send the children in to be exterminated.

The killing is described by him as follows:

> It took from three to fifteen minutes to kill the people in the death chamber. . . . We knew when the people were dead because their screaming stopped. . . . After the bodies were removed, our special commandos took off the rings and extracted the gold from the teeth of the corpses.

Rudolf Hoess reports that 2,500,000 Jews were gassed in Auschwitz.

There was no lack of heroic attempts on the part of Jews to resist this mass slaughter. The most dramatic attempt was made in the Warsaw Ghetto. How these courageous people were dealt with by the Nazis is related by SS Brigadier-General

Stroop, military commander of Warsaw, in one report dated April–May, 1943: "Countless numbers of Jews were liquidated in sewers and bunkers through blasting. . . . Police and Wehrmacht . . . discharged their duties in an exemplary manner." Stroop recorded that his action at Warsaw eliminated "a proved total of 56,065 people. To that we have to add the number of those killed through blasting, fire, etc., which cannot be counted."

According to the Nürnberg judgment: "Adolf Eichmann, who had been put in charge of this program by Hitler, has estimated that the policy pursued resulted in the killing of 6,000,000 Jews, of whom 4,000,000 were killed in the extermination institutions."

I will not go on with the descriptions of these horrors.

Now let us see what was Eichmann's role. Was he an unimportant cog in this monster machine of death and torture? No. He was in charge of this department. Wisliceny says on this subject: "Eichmann had special powers from Gruppenführer Müller, the chief of Amt IV (his immediate superior), and from the chief of the Security Police. He was responsible for the so-called solution of the Jewish question in Germany and in all countries occupied by Germany."

Bruno Waneck, another witness at the trial of the major war criminals, says:

> Eichmann occupied, already in Heydrich's lifetime, a dominant or absolute special position, constantly widening and growing, and in the whole Jewish sector he acted fully independently (meaning within the *Reichssicherheitshauptamt*). Then, after Heydrich's death till the end he was directly responsible to Himmler. This fact was, to my knowledge, generally known, within the RSHA.

An affidavit incorporated in the records of the above-mentioned trial, by Walter Huppenkothen, Gestapo officer, states:

> The Jewish section (IV B 4, later IV A 4 b) and its director, SS-Obersturmbannführer Eichmann, occupied a special posi-

tion in Amt IV. It [the section] was situated in a building on Kurfürstenstrasse, in which Eichmann and most officials of his service unit lived as well. Eichmann himself and a major portion of the officials of his service unit were not civil servants but officers of the S.D. (Security Service).

It should be noted in this connection that the so-called Jewish section and all of Amt IV were declared by the Nürnberg judgment to be a criminal organization.

And how did Eichmann carry out his task? Here is what Hoess, in his memoirs written in the Warsaw prison, says about this: "Eichmann was a vivacious, active man in his thirties, and always full of energy. He was constantly hatching new plans and perpetually on the lookout for innovations and improvements. He could never rest. He was obsessed with the Jewish question and the order which had been given for its final solution."

On an earlier conversation with Eichmann, Hoess commented as follows: "Yet even when we were quite alone together and the drink had been flowing freely so that he was in his most expansive mood, he showed that he was completely obsessed with the idea of destroying every single Jew that he could lay his hands on."

And he quotes Eichmann. Eichmann said: "Without pity and in cold blood we must complete this extermination as rapidly as possible. Any compromise, even the slightest, would have to be paid for bitterly at a later date."

Morgen, a witness for the defense at the Nürnberg trial, tells of his horror over what he found in the camps. He said:

I asked the SS Court at Berlin to investigate Eichmann on the basis of my report. The SS Court in Berlin thereupon submitted to the chief of the Reich Security Main Office, SS-Obergruppenführer Kaltenbrunner, in his capacity as highest judge, a warrant to arrest Eichmann. Dr. Bachmann reported to me that on the submission of this matter rather dramatic incidents took place. Kaltenbrunner immediately called in Müller, and now the judge was told that an arrest was in no event to be considered, for Eichmann was carrying out a special secret task of utmost importance entrusted to him by the Führer.

Wisliceny was asked: "Did he [Eichmann] say anything at that time as to the number of Jews that had been killed?" The answer was: "Yes, he expressed this in a particularly comical manner. He said he would leap laughing into the grave because the feeling that he had 5,000,000 people on his conscience would be for him a source of extraordinary satisfaction."

We are now in 1960—fifteen years after Nazi Germany was defeated. Is it not inconceivable that Eichmann has enjoyed freedom during all these years? That he has not been brought to trial? Is not this a violation of the sovereignty of the spirit of man and of humanity's conception of justice?

It is not a matter of revenge. In the words of the Hebrew poet laureate Bialik, the devil himself cannot think up a revenge for the murder of one single child. It is a matter of justice.

One of the major war criminals, Frank, governor-general of Nazi-occupied Poland, said at the Nürnberg trial: "A thousand years will pass and this guilt of Germany will not be erased." Is fifteen years long enough a period to forget? Could a Jew be expected to forget that Eichmann is still free?

What wonder that many Jews could find no rest until they ascertained whether he was alive and tracked him down. Are these the "armed bands" referred to in the statement of the representative of Argentina this morning?

I am convinced that many in the world were anxious to bring Eichmann to trial, but the fact remains that for fifteen years nobody found him. And he could break laws of who knows how many countries, by entering them under a false name and forged passport, and abuse the hospitality of countries which, I am sure, recoil in horror from his deeds. But Jews, some of whom personally are the victims of his brutality, found no rest until they located him and brought him to Israel —to the country to whose shores hundreds of thousands of the survivors of the Eichmann horror have come home; to the country that existed in the hearts and minds of the 6,000,000, as on the way to the crematoria they chanted the great article of our Faith: *Ani maamin be'emuna shlema beviat haMashiah* —"I believe with perfect faith in the coming of the Messiah."

A considerable part of the address we heard this morning was devoted to elaborating the charge that the state of Israel has violated the sovereignty of Argentina. I emphatically deny this charge. The state of Israel has not violated the sovereignty of Argentina in any manner, and there is nothing in the record to enable the Security Council to make any such findings. The government of Israel has made clear in official communications to the Argentine government, which appear now on the record of the Security Council, that certain of its nationals in the course of their efforts to bring Eichmann to justice may have committed infringement of the law of Argentina, and it has already twice expressed its regret for this. I wish to repeat in all solemnity before this Council my government's regrets at any infringement of the law of Argentina which may have been committed by any national of Israel. But with the greatest respect for the representative of Argentina, I think that he is in complete error, as a basic legal proposition, in confusing the illegal actions of individuals, for which regrets have been expressed, with the nonexistent intentional violation of the sovereignty of one member state by another. This distinction is so fundamental and so well established in international law that I am at a complete loss to understand how it could be expected that the Security Council should make so far-reaching a finding as is implicit in the statement we heard this morning, without any adequate basis in fact and in law.

Again I want to stress that if citizens of Israel broke the law of Argentina, they broke it not in tracking down any ordinary criminal, but in tracking down Adolf Eichmann. And here I must ask, would Argentina have admitted Adolf Eichmann into its territory had it known his true identity? Would asylum have been accorded him? Surely not.

The representative of Argentina expressed anxiety that this, if not dealt with by the Security Council, might constitute a precedent. But modern history knows few monsters such as

Adolf Eichmann. The representative of Argentina has sought to contrast the norms of ordinary legal procedure, on the one hand, with resort to lynching and mob violence on the other. Insofar as he sought, in the latter connection, to draw an analogy to the apprehension of Eichmann, there is no analogy. Far from lynching Eichmann or hanging him on the nearest tree, those who pursued him over fifteen years and finally seized him have handed him over to the process and judgment of the courts of law. The reference to mob passions and lawless justice in this context, I must say, is unwarranted and provocative. This is not only my view and that of the government of Israel; it is also shared by prominent people all over the world. In an article by a well-known Argentine publicist, Ernesto Sabato, published in the important newspaper *El Mundo* of 17 June, under the suggestive title "Sovereignty for Butchers," we read: "How can we not admire a group of brave men who have, during the years, endangered their lives in searching throughout the world for this criminal and who had yet the honesty to deliver him up for trial by judicial tribunals instead of being impelled by an impulse of revenge to finish him off on the spot."

Will not our Argentine friends see the exceptional nature and uniqueness of this case? I am sure that their conception of right and justice must place this isolated incident in its proper perspective.

I again ask: is this a problem for the Security Council to deal with? This is a body that deals with threats to the peace. Is this a threat to peace—Eichmann brought to trial by the very people to whose total physical annihilation he dedicated all his energies, even if the manner of his apprehension violated the laws of Argentina? Or did the threat to peace lie in Eichmann at large, Eichmann unpunished, Eichmann free to spread the poison of his twisted soul to a new generation?

16. Toward a Solution of the Arab Refugee Problem

A statement by Mrs. Meir in the Special Political Committee of the General Assembly. (In English, December 15, 1961)

In their speeches Arab spokesmen have been trying to assert that Israel is not a nation; that the Jews are not a people; that the Jews have no real connection with the Holy Land; that Zionism is a sinister imperialist conspiracy; that the United Nations had no right to take the decision in 1947; that it was not the Arabs who had attacked Israel after the decision.

May I suggest that representatives of the Arab countries not lecture us on the question of whether we are a people or a race or a religion, but leave it to us to find our own way toward a secure future out of the hardships, sufferings, and miseries that fate imposed upon us throughout the centuries? It is perhaps difficult for some to grasp this strange phenomenon of Jewish history. The Jewish people is four thousand years old. The origin of its history and of its spiritual creation is linked with the land of the Bible. In antiquity the Jewish state was destroyed by powerful neighbors. The Jews went into exile, only to return centuries later and establish a state once more. Centuries later the state was again conquered by more powerful foes after long years of war, and the Jews again went into exile, this time in a dispersion which scattered them to all parts of the globe.

Yet during all these generations Jews in their worldwide dispersion clung to the idea of returning one day to the land which was the one place on the globe associated with their history and with the spiritual heritage which they gave to the whole of mankind. Never for a day did the Jews cease to pray for and dream about the return to the land from which their people had sprung, the land in which they had accepted the concept of one God; the land in which their Prophets had proclaimed the vision of the brotherhood of man, of justice, and of universal peace. Throughout the generations some Jews continued to live in Palestine. Over and over again Jews from various parts of the world came back, some driven by anti-Semitism and persecution, and many impelled by their need for the renaissance of a national life with dignity and self-expression. Throughout the ages, although Jews lived as minorities in many countries and were engulfed by the languages and culture of others, their Hebrew language never died. The people remained alive, their ancient language, the language of the Bible, was kept alive, and so was their faith in their ultimate return to the land of their fathers.

Although at various stages our land was conquered and occupied by mighty foreign empires, the Jewish people never submitted to their rule. Historical records, now supplemented by archaeological discoveries all over the Middle East, bear testimony to Israel's rebellions against foreign rulers and its struggle for independence. For generation upon generation, throughout the centuries, Jews turned toward Jerusalem in their daily devotions, and the words of the Psalmist, "If I forget thee, O Jerusalem," have become perhaps the most essential tenet of Judaism. The Bible set the distinctive course of Israel and of the land of Israel in human history, a course of interlocked and lasting destiny.

A passage from the official report of the Palestine Royal Commission of July, 1937, reads:

While the Jews had thus been dispersed over the world, they have never forgotten Palestine. If Christians have become familiar through the Bible with the physiognomy of the country and its place, names and events that happened more than two thousand years ago, the link which binds the Jews to Palestine and its past history is to them far closer and more intimate. Judaism and its ritual are rooted in those memories. Among countless illustrations it is enough to cite the fact that Jews, wherever they may be, still pray for rain at the season it is needed in Palestine. And the same devotion to the Land of Israel, Eretz Israel, the same sense of exile from it, permeates Jewish secular thought. Some of the finest Hebrew poetry written in the diaspora has been inspired like the Psalms of the Captivity by the longing to return to Zion.

Nor has the link been merely spiritual or intellectual. Always or almost always since the fall of the Jewish State, some Jews have been living in Palestine. Under Arab rule there were substantial Jewish communities in the chief towns. In the period of the Crusades and again in the Mongol invasions, they were nearly but not entirely blotted out. Under Ottoman rule they slowly recovered. Fresh immigrants arrived from time to time, from Spain in the sixteenth century, from Eastern Europe in the seventeenth. They settled mainly in Galilee, in numerous villages spreading northwards to the Lebanon and in the towns of Safad and Tiberias. Safad, which according to Jewish tradition contained as many as 15,000 Jews in the sixteenth century, became a centre of Rabbinical learning and exercised a profound influence on Jewish thought throughout the diaspora.

The report continues:

Small though their numbers were, the continued existence of those Jews in Palestine meant much to all Jewry. Multitudes of poor Jews and ignorant Jews in the ghettos of Eastern Europe felt themselves represented, as it were, by this remnant of their race who were keeping a foothold in the land against the day of the coming of the Messiah.

This belief in the divine promise of eventual return to

Palestine largely accounts for the steadfastness with which the Jews of the diaspora clung to their faith and endured persecution.

What wonder then that down the ages this unique phenomenon has inspired men of vision to support the restoration of the Jewish people to its land.

The recognition of this fundamental truth was the cause for the Balfour Declaration, for the League of Nations Mandate, for the support that we have enjoyed throughout the years from many men and women of different faiths throughout the world, and finally for the resolution of the United Nations to establish a Jewish state in part of Palestine. No oratory and no vituperation can change these historic facts.

After World War I, this historic connection between the Jewish people and their land was formally recognized, first by Great Britain and later by international society as it was then organized in the League of Nations. The purpose of the mandate for Palestine was clearly stated as being the reconstitution of the Jewish National Home in that country. The text of the mandate recognizes and reaffirms the historic connection of the Jewish people with Palestine. The very term "Jewish National Home" denotes the recognition on the part of the League of Nations that the Jews have national rights in that country. Of course, it was realized that there was an Arab population living there, and we accepted the proviso that in reestablishing the Jewish national home nothing should be done that might be injurious to the civil and religious rights of the non-Jewish population. A clear distinction was drawn between the national rights of the Jewish people in Palestine, on the one hand, and the civil and religious rights of the Arab population, on the other. In that way Palestine was set aside for the Jewish national home at a time when that same League of Nations decided that the major part of the area which we now call the Middle or Near East would be advanced toward independence for the Arab peoples. At that time not a single Arab state existed in the area.

Arab representatives talk here as though the establishment of the Jewish national home and of the state of Israel had deprived the Arab nation of national independence. In fact, what the League of Nations decided at that time, and what the United Nations later confirmed anew in 1947, was the concept that side by side with the Arab people achieving independence in the wide expanses of the Middle East, the Jewish people should be allowed to rebuild its own national future in the tiny land set aside for it. Has not this concept come to abundant fulfillment?

What was the political landscape in the Middle East before the First World War? The area that is now Israel, Jordan, Syria, and the Lebanon were vilayets of the Syrian Province of the Ottoman Empire. What is today Iraq and the independent states in the Arabian Peninsula were also provinces of that empire. Only in the framework of the political settlement after the First World War did a pattern of new territorial entities emerge.

It is interesting to remember that those territories which are now independent Arab states have become such as a result of what the Arab delegations have described here as "imperialist machinations." With the dismemberment of the Ottoman Empire, and only then, did Palestine become a separate political entity designated by the League of Nations in 1921 to contain the national home of the Jewish people. In the White Paper of 1922, Mr. Churchill limited the territory to which the Jewish national home provisions of the mandate applied to the land situated west of the Jordan River, *i.e.,* to less than one-fourth of the original area of the mandate. In 1947 this latter area, by the Resolution of the United Nations of 29 November, was further partitioned. The state of Israel today has about 8,000 square miles; the area in the Middle East in which the Arab States have gained their independence since the end of the First World War covers over 3,000,000 square miles.

In the presence of so many Arab representatives, it is really rather a mockery to state that the reestablishment of Jewish independence in a tiny corner of the Middle East has robbed the

Arab nation of independence. It was considered just and fair, in international equity, that side by side with the independent Arab states that were to arise and did arise, there would also arise a Jewish state.

At the end of World War I the then Arab leadership accepted this plan and welcomed the return of the Jews to Palestine. If Arab leadership had remained faithful to the concept of good neighborliness between emerging Arab states in the Middle East and the state of Israel, then the world would have been spared all this misery, and the Arabs of Palestine would have lived with us in the national home and in the state of Israel without any of the difficulties that ensued.

But Arab leadership did not reconcile itself to the verdict of the community of nations, and political strife in Palestine began. Finally, the problem was put to the United Nations, the successor of the League of Nations. Again the judgment of the international community was to confirm Jewish national rights in that country. By way of a compromise solution, the United Nations decided after thorough investigation and prolonged discussion, to partition Palestine so that in one part of the country a Jewish state would arise and in the other part yet another Arab state would be created. This is the essence of the United Nations Resolution of November, 1947.

Of course, we proceeded to organize our defensive capacity in the country. What else were we to do in the face of the decision taken by the Arab states to undo the United Nations Resolution by means of war? We appealed to the Arabs of Palestine and to the Arab states to accept the verdict of the United Nations. The Arab states, however, urged the Arabs of Palestine not to accept the United Nations Resolution, incited them to rise against the Jews in the country, sent to their aid irregular armed forces, and promised them that as soon as the British would leave the country, they would march in with their regular armies in order to crush the Jewish state. During the period between the adoption of the United Nations Resolution in November, 1947, and the end of the British mandate in May, 1948, the Arabs of Palestine, encouraged and militarily reinforced by the Arab states, began all-out attacks against Jewish towns and villages. There is not a shred of evidence in United Nations documents to substantiate the false charge made by the representative of Iraq that it was the Jews who, on the morrow of the United Nations decision, proceeded to attack the Arab community and to take over the whole country. Precisely the contrary is true. We have shown how, immediately after the decision was taken, the Arab states announced from the rostrum of the United Nations that they would never accept it and that they would fight it by every means at their disposal. We appealed for acceptance and peace. They decided on rejection and war, and thus hostilities in Palestine began. Naturally, we defended ourselves.

I must again quote what the United Nations Palestine Commission said on this point on 16 February, 1948: "Powerful Arab interests both inside and outside Palestine are defying the resolution of the General Assembly and are engaged in a deliberate effort to alter by force the settlement envisaged therein."

On 15 May, 1948, the British left, and the Arab armies invaded the country. Already, by that time, hundreds of thousands of Palestine Arabs had left their homes and had become refugees as a result of the fighting that had taken place in the country, in consequence of the Arab onslaught on the Jewish community. When the regular Arab armies joined the fighting and full-scale war ensued, the number of refugees swelled. By the time the war was over and the Arab armies had been beaten back the refugee problem had come into being.

Every modern war creates a refugee problem. The responsibility, however, for the fact that Arabs became refugees must squarely lie with those who, instead of accepting the verdict of the United Nations, went to war to undo it and perpetrated the aggression of 15 May, 1948, against the state of Israel. Large numbers of the refugees left the country at the call of the Arab leaders, who told them to get out so that Arab armies could get in.

Arab representatives stressed the tragedy of Deir Yassin, where civilian Arabs were murdered by a Jewish dissident group. This action was at once disavowed and condemned by the official Jewish leadership. Those who perpetrated these murders certainly sinned heavily against the standards of self-defense which the Jewish community had set itself. Yet at the same time, it is historically incorrect to state that the exodus of the Arab refugees was due to this tragic incident.

Without in any way detracting from the condemnation of what occurred at Deir Yassin, I cannot altogether pass in silence over some of the grave outrages perpetrated at the time by the other side. We cannot forget the assault on the medical convoy on its way to the Hadassah Hospital on Mount Scopus in Jerusalem, when seventy-seven doctors and nurses were killed in cold blood. We cannot forget how the period beginning twenty-four hours after the United Nations Resolution was characterized by the daily toll of innocent lives of Jews traveling in the country. The road to Jerusalem is still today flanked by burned-out cars whose peaceful passengers fell victim to organized Arab ambush and terror. I shall not give a long list of such instances, but I would like to find one statement of responsible Arab leaders denouncing the massacre of medical personnel and other civilians.

If the Arab states had accepted the United Nations Resolution and if they had urged the Arabs of Palestine to do likewise, instead of inciting them to fight in order to undo the resolution, there would have been no bloodshed and not a single refugee. The Jewish and Arab States in Palestine would have arisen in peace and cooperation and subsequent history would have been different. Indeed, some 100,000 Arabs did not join the general flight and remained within Israel. Since then their number has risen through natural increase and through the return of some refugees from beyond the frontiers, and today there are a quarter of a million Arabs in Israel.

Some of the stock allegations of the Arab representatives pertain to the situation of the Arab population of Israel. These allegations are as malicious as they are unfounded, and my colleagues and I have on many occasions refuted them. Suffice it to say, at this time, that the Arabs of Israel share to the fullest the rights of every citizen of the country. They take part in the elections along with all other citizens; they are represented in the Knesset (the Israel Parliament); they take an active part in all walks of life—they are judges and mayors, doctors and lawyers, teachers and social workers. They enjoy standards of living in health, welfare, and education unequaled in any Arab state. We are proud of their important contribution to the development of the country.

I must now dwell on the numbers of Arab refugees. There is no doubt about the present UNRWA rolls being inflated. There are not a million-odd bona fide refugees, and there never were. On 31 December, 1946, according to the figures supplied by the government of Palestine to UNSCOP, the total number of Arabs in unpartitioned Palestine was 1,288,000. Of this number were resident in the former mandated territory, later annexed by Jordan, about 500,000. In the area later annexed by Egypt—namely, the Gaza Strip—there were over 100,000. Furthermore, about 100,000 Arabs never left the area which is now Israel, and a further 40,000 returned to Israel. The total of Arabs, therefore, who left the area which is Israel could not have exceeded 540,000 to 550,000.

As the Commissioner-General has pointed out, at least 20 percent were immediately absorbed and never became dependent on UNRWA. This should have left about 400,000 genuine refugees on the rolls. But, as United Nations documents indicate, the original lists of relief recipients in 1948–49 included not only refugees, but also a large proportion of impoverished local inhabitants. On 4 November, 1949, the Secretary-General submitted to the Assembly a "Report of Assistance to Palestine Refugees." In a passage headed "Difficulty of Definition" this report describes the haphazard way in which the relief rolls were compiled, the lack of any eligibility test, and the extreme difficulty in practice to distinguish between persons displaced from their homes as a result of hostilities, indigent or unemployed local residents, and nomadic and seminomadic Bedouin who would naturally gather at places where food was being distributed. The Secretary-General added that a considerable percentage of the refugees were in small villages where the food was being distributed by the local mayor, and it could not be doubted that in many cases individuals who could not qualify as being "bona fide" refugees were in fact on relief rolls. In the same year, 1949, the Final Report of the United Nations Economic Survey Commission to the Middle East (the Clapp Report) estimated that at least 160,000 nonrefugees had managed to get on to the relief rolls.

During the years since then, as has often been pointed out in UNRWA reports, the figures have become even more inflated. In Table 1, annexed to this year's Report, a footnote warns: "The above statistics are based on the Agency's registration records which do not necessarily reflect the actual refugee population owing to factors such as the high rate of unreported deaths and undetected false registrations."

In addition, the agency has no adequate machinery for checking which of the refugees have become wholly or partly self-supporting. This would in any circumstances not have been easy to find out, since only 40 percent of the refugees live in camps. A substantial measure of "spontaneous absorption," taking place in Jordan, Syria and Lebanon, is not adequately reflected in UNRWA statistics.

These are some of the factors which explain the inflation of the rolls. The agency claims that since 1950, more than 425,000 names have been removed from the rolls through routine processes. A good part of those names must relate to "bona fide" refugees registered in 1949, who, as we have pointed out, were about 400,000. Naturally, there is a fair margin of error in any such calculations. But, even allowing for natural increase, it is clear that only a part of UNRWA's present grand total of 1,174,760 falls within the accepted definition of Palestinian refugees. The rectification of the rolls has come up repeatedly in annual reports and Assembly resolutions, but it has not been carried out due to the opposition of the host governments.

This analysis does not bear out the political contentions of Arab spokesmen. It is always a human tragedy when people are uprooted and displaced from their homes, for whatever reason, and all of us must view the problem of these refugees with compassion and a desire to help them. It is a different matter when the problem is presented to us in political terms as that of a whole nation which has been deprived of its national homeland. The great majority of the Arab inhabitants of what was formerly Palestine have remained within the former area of the mandated territory. Part of them are Arabs whose former homes were within the present frontiers of Israel, and part of them are Arabs whose former homes were and still are in districts now occupied by Jordan, where they have become citizens, as well as districts occupied by the United Arab Republic.

We are today faced with an Arab refugee problem as a result of the war which the Arab states launched against Israel in 1947 and 1948. This has remained the only group of refugees whose lot has not been eased by their own kinsmen. Many millions of other refugees, displaced as a result of wars and upheavals, have been received and rehabilitated by their people and been permitted to lead a normal life amongst them. In some instances the solution lay in an exchange of populations, as in the case of Greece and Turkey. The Arab refugee problem is the only instance where out of political considerations, hundreds of thousands of people are compelled to remain refugees, denied natural acceptance by their own kinsmen. How can one reconcile the outcry over the fate of the refugees living on international charity with the fierce opposition to any plan of constructive development, of resettlement and of integration designed to rehabilitate these unfortunate people?

I mentioned that in some cases the solution lay in an exchange of population. I should like to emphasize the fact that we in Israel have received since 1948 over 500,000 Jewish refugees from the Arab countries—that is, practically the same number as that of Arabs who left the area which is Israel.

These Jewish refugees from Arab states and their children comprise a very substantial part of Israel's total population. A striking indication of this lies in the fact that no less than 55 percent of the children of grade-school age in Israel are from

families who came to Israel from the countries which are mem
bers of the Arab League.

On their arrival in Israel the occupational structure of these
Jewish refugees was heavily imbalanced. Less than 1 percent of
them in their countries of origin had been engaged in agricul
ture; less than 2 percent had been engaged in the building
trades; a very substantial percentage were illiterate. The vast
majority could be absorbed initially only in unskilled work, and
nearly all had to be taught new trades and occupations before
they could be fully integrated into the country's growing
economy.

Our approach to these refugees was that they were our
brothers and sisters; that they must be given full equality, not
just in theory but in practice; that they must be helped to take
a productive part in our economy and our public life; and that
their children in particular must be helped quickly to move
upwards on the educational ladder so that within as short a
period as possible they would reach the general level.

Of course, this policy could not be carried out without what
has been referred to as "uneconomic" expenditure. I think that
these expenditures produce the greatest economic asset that any
society could possibly wish for or possess—namely, human be-
ings who have regained their dignity, who realize the extent of
their God-given capacities and are filled with the desire to
express those capacities in their own interests and in the interest
of the society of which they are part.

As a result of this attitude toward these refugees and of the
determination to help them transform themselves as rapidly
as possible into productive citizens, we have seen this growing
section of our population change with striking speed. Those
who were unemployable on their arrival are today gainfully
employed in agriculture, industry, mining, communications,
and services. Those who needed assistance upon their arrival
for their most elementary needs of shelter, medical care, food,
clothing, and education today are making their full contribution
as self-supporting citizens to the common good.

I do not think that we in Israel are unique in this respect. I could mention a number of countries which in the period since the end of World War II have reacted in the same way to the human challenge of refugee populations of their own kinsmen, both in Europe and in Asia. We have listened with interest to what the distinguished representative of Greece has told the committee about the reception centers for Greek refugees arriving in his country since 1957. It is not without significance that precisely where such an attitude had been displayed it has resulted not only in a transformation of refugees into citizens, but also in the economic growth and development of the countries receiving them.

The eyes of the refugee should be directed toward the future, toward the opportunities present in his existing environment to which he is closely linked by ties of language, culture, faith, and customs.

The central aspect of the Arab presentations which we have heard during the debate this year, as on so many previous occasions, is that the refugee is used as a political instrument for the attainment of negative and destructive objectives which we have heard defined in terms diametrically opposed to the letter and spirit of the Charter of the United Nations. I have no doubt what members of the United Nations think of these objectives or of the spirit which advances them. It breeds not peace, but war. It is a spirit which does not solve refugee problems but which, if permitted to express itself in action, would create only additional human misery in the entire area.

I am certain that after hearing the speeches of representatives of the Arab states and of the refugee spokesmen, no delegate here can have any doubt as to the real purpose of the Arab states—which is not to allow the creation of normal and peaceful conditions between themselves and Israel—or as to the real desires of the refugees—which is not to return to Israel as loyal citizens of the country. As I have said at the outset, the purpose of the Arab states is to achieve the destruction of Israel, and the immediate repatriation of hundreds of thousands of anti-Israelis into Israel is designed to soften up Israel, from within, toward her final elimination. There are dozens of speeches, dozens of broadcasts and dozens of articles by Arab leaders in every Arab country that say quite clearly that the repatriation of the refugees is a means toward the destruction of Israel. I give here but one example. In an interview on a German television service, reproduced in the Swiss newspaper *Zuercher Woche* of 1 September, 1961, President Nasser of Egypt says: "When the Arabs return to Israel, Israel will cease to exist." Distinguished delegates will not be surprised that we are not prepared to cooperate in this scheme.

Is it not perfectly obvious that the representatives of the Arab states are not really searching for a solution of the refugee problem but for the dissolution of the state of Israel? They themselves say that they are trying to secure their return into Israel within the context of the proposition that Israel has no right to exist and must be eliminated.

We in Israel are very sensitive to the fact that there are hundreds of thousands of people living the lives of refugees and subsisting on international charity. My people know what it is to be a refugee. We are concerned about the future of these people, and we believe that the United Nations and this committee should address themselves to the question, what is the best way of securing a better future for every one of them. In fact, we have done certain things ourselves in this matter to alleviate the Arab refugee situation. Since the end of the fighting, about 40,000 Arabs have come back into the country and have been integrated with the community; several thousands of these came under the scheme providing for the reunion of families which had been broken up by the fighting.

Ever since 1949, we have declared our willingness to pay compensation for refugee property abandoned in Israel. We stated our readiness to pay such compensation even before a settlement of all other outstanding issues—provided, of course, that such funds be used as part of an overall plan for the solution of the refugee problem. If this has not yet been effectuated, it is due to the fact that the Arab countries have insisted on immediate repatriation and have spurned those offers. In any negotiations about compensation we reserve the right to bring up the question of compensation for the property of Israeli citizens which was confiscated when they left Arab countries, as well as for the property abandoned by Jews during the war of 1948 in parts of the country which was annexed by Jordan, such as the Jewish Quarter of the Old City of Jerusalem, and elsewhere.

In response to requests made by the Conciliation Commission, the government of Israel agreed to release all blocked bank accounts and safe deposits left behind by refugees in banks in Israel. In doing so, my government desired to make a contribution of goodwill to alleviate the lot of a considerable number of refugees and to further the advance of peaceful relations between Israel and the Arab states. Under the first release scheme, a sum of 740,000 pounds sterling was transferred to their owners, residing in Arab countries or elsewhere. Under a second release scheme another 2,800,000 pounds sterling were transferred. A sum total of more than 3,500,000 pounds sterling flowed from Israel into the coffers of the Arab states, notwithstanding the fact that they were maintaining their practices of economic warfare and blockade in exercise of an alleged state of war, in flagrant violation of the United Nations Charter.

The Conciliation Commission in its Twelfth Progress Report hailed that unilateral action of Israel on behalf of the refugees "as an important step towards the settlement of the differences existing between Israel and her neighbors." Yet, to our regret, this act, which was undertaken by Israel without any conditions and which, in the light of the prevailing circumstances, was a unique gesture, did in no instance evoke any pacific or constructive reaction on the part of the Arab governments. Worse than that, they even put up obstacles to frustrate the implementation of this release scheme.

Let us now contrast this with the attitude of the Arab governments toward creating a future for those who became refugees in the first place as a result of the disastrous decision of the Arab leaders to go to war. They have constantly rejected any plan which, if implemented, would have absorbed large numbers of refugees. They rejected the Clapp Report—the Report of the United Nations Economic Survey Mission for the Middle

East of 1949—which recommended an economic approach to the problem and the gradual integration of the refugees in the expanding economy of the area.

In 1959 the late Secretary-General, Mr. Hammarskjöld, enlarged on this concept in his proposals to the General Assembly, where he recommended a large-scale development plan for the Middle East, within which the refugees would find a constructive future. Can anyone doubt the need for such a project? His plan, if executed, would have brought about a far-reaching transformation of this underdeveloped area and would have resulted in the absorption of large numbers of refugees. The Arab states would not hear of such a plan. According to their book, nothing must be done, and the refugees must continue to linger in their camps in order to be kept as a permanent threat against Israel.

In 1953 the United States government attempted to bring about the implementation of a regional irrigation project. Such a scheme would have been of enormous benefit to Jordan, to Israel, and in part also to Syria. For two years, the representative of President Eisenhower, Mr. Eric Johnston, negotiated with the Arab states and with Israel and finally succeeded in working out a plan for water distribution that was agreed upon by both Arab and Israel experts. The Israel government accepted the plan. The Arab politicians vetoed it. If implemented, it would have enabled about a quarter of a million refugees to resettle in homes on irrigated land and to lead a normal and productive existence. But again this was not to be. The overriding consideration is not what is good for the refugee, but what is detrimental to Israel. On 19 October, 1958, Mr. Johnston wrote in the *New York Times Magazine*: "After two years of discussion, technical experts of Israel, Jordan, Lebanon and Syria agreed upon every important detail of a unified Jordan plan. But in October 1955, it was rejected for political reasons at a meeting of the Arab League."

Similarly, Syria frustrated the efforts of UNRWA in 1951 and 1952 to develop rehabilitation projects in that country. Egypt withdrew her earlier agreement to a plan for the settlement of 70,000 refugees on lands to be irrigated in the Sinai Peninsula. These two instances are mentioned in the Report of the Director of UNWRA for the year 1954–1955. · · ·

The underlying causes for these negative Arab policies were recently again depicted in a series of articles published in the noted Swiss daily *Neue Zuercher Zeitung* by Arnold Hottinger, who is a prominent Swiss authority on Near Eastern affairs. He says:

> The "Palestine Specialists" who exist in all Arab countries, and who are always called upon when refugee problems are discussed on the political level, are well-to-do, well established Palestinians. . . . They have succeeded in asserting their opinions on Palestine questions as the only one acceptable, and they watch carefully lest any Arab deviate from this line and be it only by the breadth of a hair. The opinion of these "specialists" who themselves do not suffer any personal hardship from their refugee status, is easy to summarize: The refugees are to be left in their miserable condition as a sort of pawn for Arab rights in Palestine; it is not desirable that they adapt themselves to the economic life of their Arab host countries, because that would mean the loss of the strongest lever by which the Arabs hope to move the world once more to put the Palestine question on the agenda.

This is the considered opinion of a neutral observer with long-standing experience in Near Eastern affairs. The best corroboration for these views are the speeches which we heard here from the Arab representatives.

If only the 40,000,000 Arabs had done for their refugees what the 650,000 Jews who were in Israel in 1948 did for 1,000,000 Jewish refugees—including half a million from Arab countries —who have been integrated with us since then! We shared our resources with them. We introduced severe rationing and strict austerity measures. Of course, we received aid from friendly governments, as do all newly emerging states, but aid came chiefly from Jews the world over, because there is Jewish brotherhood. Certainly, Jews in the United States and elsewhere have a deep affection for the state of Israel. This lessens to no degree their loyalty to and citizenship of the countries in which they reside. But Jews all over the world care what happens to their fellow Jews who are refugees, and they organize in order to assist them to rebuild their lives in Israel. We cared for our refugees in such a way that they have now become builders of a modern, developing country.

The Arab refugees are not in strange and foreign lands. They are Arabs in Arab countries, amongst their own kith and kin, in a familiar environment of language, history, background, customs, and religion. Would it not have been the most natural thing in the world for the Arab countries to do as we did— namely, to take in their brethren and create a new life for them within their vast expanses, with international aid, including compensation for property from Israel, and within the framework of the economic development of those countries? In various parts of the world, tens of millions of people who became refugees as a result of fighting or political upheavals have been constructively resettled among their own kith and kin in neighboring lands, and the practical problem before us is in no way unique. Where is the brotherly care on the part of the Arab countries for the refugees? I am not referring to politics, but to simple human brotherhood.

The representative of Iraq argued that the issue is not between the Arab states and Israel, but between Israel and the Arab refugees from Palestine. In the same breath he based himself on United Nations resolutions. Let it clearly be stated that all United Nations resolutions on this subject recognize the Arab states and the state of Israel as parties to the dispute, and, as I have mentioned, many resolutions have called on these two parties to enter into negotiations and resolve their differences. This unfortunate conflict is between Israel and the Arab states who refuse to establish peaceful relations with her and who refuse to cooperate in solving the refugee problem within the context of the restoration of peace in the area.

It has been said here that negotiations are useless because the positions of the parties are firmly stated and they are far apart.

That is precisely why negotiations are needed. Despite our disappointments and despite the venom and abuse hurled at us, we remain convinced that negotiations are the only way. Unfortunately, for the time being there is little hope that the Arab states will accept such an approach, for they have chosen in this very committee to reject negotiations and have threatened to force their solution upon us by war.

I should now like to sum up the position of my government as follows:

(1) We accepted the 1947 compromise solution. Had the Arab states done likewise and urged the Arabs of Palestine to do so, there would have been a Jewish state and an Arab state living together in peace and cooperation.

(2) The Arab states instead decided to launch a war against Israel. The Arab refugee problem arose as a consequence of this war. Those responsible for that war are responsible for the existence of the refugee problem.

(3) About 550,000 Arabs left the territory which is now Israel. A similar number of Jewish refugees from the Arab countries have since been integrated into Israel. There has thus been a *de facto* exchange of population.

(4) No United Nations resolution demands immediate, total, and unconditional repatriation of refugees into Israel. On the other hand, there are United Nations resolutions calling for negotiations of the peaceful settlement of all outstanding questions.

(5) Israel believes that the future of the Arab refugees lies in their resettlement in the Arab countries, within the framework of the economic development of the Middle East.

(6) Israel stands by its readiness to pay compensation for property abandoned by the refugees, even before a general peace settlement is concluded—provided these funds are used for the overall solution of the problem. Israel will demand compensation for property of its citizens that was confiscated by the Arab governments.

We feel certain that despite the present hostility, which prevents the solution of the refugee problem and of other problems outstanding between us and our neighbors, the day will come when Arab leadership will realize the futility of their present attitude.

My country remains ready at all times to put aside the rancors of the past and to work out with the Arab leaders a better future for the Middle East as a whole, where there will be development, freedom and happiness for the Arab states, as well as for Israel, in which those who are now refugees will fully share.

17. In the Hour of Deliverance: 1967

Immediately upon the close of hostilities in the Six-Day War Mrs. Meir arrived in New York to fulfill a speaking engagement made months before. Coming straight from the plane, she addressed a huge rally of the United Jewish Appeal at Madison Square Garden. As usual she spoke extemporaneously. (In English, June 11, 1967)

Once again we have won a war, the third in a very brief history of independence. The last thing that Israelis want is to win wars. We don't want wars. We want peace more than all else. But our Arab neighbors and our neighbors' friends must learn this lesson. Those that perished in Hitler's gas chambers were the last Jews to die without standing up to defend themselves. Helpless Jewish victims tried to fight in the Warsaw Ghetto, the Vilna Ghetto, in Bialystok, but they were empty-handed, with only their spirit against Hitler's tanks.

A few weeks ago, before the outbreak of the Six-Day War, Chief of Staff Itzhak Rabin, addressing a large meeting on Independence Day, recalled his experiences as a young Palmach commander, some twenty years ago, during Israel's War of Independence in 1948. He told of one day when most of the men in his command fell in battle, and the reserves sent to him consisted of youngsters fifteen and sixteen years old with few weapons. They sat around that evening and debated whether they should give up. They decided to hold out one more day—a day that proved decisive in our favor. On that day, Rabin took an oath swearing that if he ever were able to influence the security of Israel, he would do all in his power so that Israel would never again face her enemies on such unequal terms.

This oath of Rabin's has been fulfilled, but at a price. We are a small people of only 2,500,000, surrounded by tens of millions of Arabs. We have to pay for the arms we buy, and we give thanks to any government that consents to sell us the guns, tanks, or planes we must have. Our neighbors, on the other hand, have a supplier that is always at their beck and call. We are told that Egypt, alone, lost three and a half billion dollars' worth of arms in this war that lasted a few hours.

Nasser did not pay for these weapons. And I am very much afraid that they will be replaced. I am afraid, not because I fear that we will be conquered in a new war, but because we don't want war! We do not want to spend the little we have, get, or earn for tanks and planes. We have more significant tasks to perform.

Nevertheless, if we had ten years of relative peace—we called it peace despite the incidents on the borders, the boys killed at the kibbutz of Almagor, the railroad mined, the cars blown up by mines—it was because Nasser was convinced that he was not yet strong enough to attack Israel.

This June he made his big mistake. He thought he was strong enough. He counted strength merely by the numbers of his men, his tanks, his planes, and he thought that, in view of his preponderance in arms and manpower, he was now strong enough. He forgot one element—the spirit of a small people whose only alternative to repulsing the foe was to be driven into the Mediterranean.

This people did not fight for territorial expansion. Our boys were not sent to battle as were the Egyptian soldiers in a "holy war" to destroy and annihilate. Our soldiers went to battle so that people should live! They were sent by a government who they knew was prepared and is prepared at any moment for peace and cooperation with its Arab neighbors and for peace with the entire world.

For weeks the Sinai Desert, the same desert we were forced to evacuate in 1957 though we had won, was filled with tens of thousands of Egyptian soldiers, with over a thousand tanks and vast stores of ammunition. So was the Gaza Strip. In 1957 we had been promised that if we evacuated Gaza, Egyptian soldiers would never enter Gaza. They returned a few hours after we left Gaza. Sharm el-Sheikh, the waterway to Elath, was closed by Nasser. This took place after the family of nations, especially all the maritime countries, had solemnly promised that this waterway would offer free passage to Israel vessels as to other ships. But when Nasser decided to close the straits, they remained closed.

We know that we have good friends in the world. Americans are privileged to live in a country considered by us as one of the greatest friends of Israel. We have other friends as well. And yet we had to go it alone. We did not want anybody to go to war for us. We did not want one drop of blood spilled by anybody else for our freedom and for our survival. We waited, day after day, for more than two weeks, while this huge apparatus for killing and destruction massing on our border became more menacing.

We were hoping against hope that perhaps this time something would be done by the great powers to prevent the war. Until last Monday morning—it seems as though it was years ago—Nasser's soldiers kept moving closer and closer to our borders; his planes in the Sinai were only minutes away from Tel Aviv. Thank God, that our airfields were not knocked out first, but that our air force was quick and effective enough to knock out the airfields and the planes of Egypt in the first few hours.

We never intended to shoot a single bullet over the Jordanian border. But when King Hussein saw fit to join Nasser in attack because he was evidently misled by Nasser's statement that the Egyptian dictator was now strong enough to destroy Israel, when he sought to take part in the sure victory against Israel, when

Hussein's army began to fight around the walls of Jerusalem up to Mea Shearim, when every settlement on the borders of Jordan was shelled, Hussein became an enemy who had to be repelled, and he was.

Syria believed for a long time that its guns on the top of the Golan Heights, pointed at our villages in the valley below, would assure it victory. The Syrians were mistaken. Not only the soldiers in Sinai and in the Israel Army should be considered heroes. So should the men and women and children in the valley, who did not budge from Ein Gev, from al-Magor, Tel Katzir, Gadot, Lahavot Habashan, and Dan. In all those exposed villages in the valley, not one mother took her baby and left. They remained under tons of Syrian shellings; they remained in the south, in the Negev, near the Gaza Strip. Yet many of those mothers had recently come into the country. Among those that arrived after the Second World War many had lost their children in the gas chambers of the Nazi death camps; they now have children that have grown up in Israel. These mothers let their sons go to battle, without an arm outstretched to hold them back. They watched them go, firm not only in the consciousness that this was the only hope for the 2,000,000 Jews of Israel, but in the knowledge that no Jew in the world would feel free, if we did not maintain our freedom, at any cost, in Israel.

I left Israel Friday noon. I could not bear the thought of leaving Israel without going to the Western Wall, now that it was at last possible to go there after twenty years, so I went early Friday morning. The first time I had come to the Western Wall was exactly forty-six years ago when I arrived from the United States to the then Palestine. Every Jewish child has heard about the *Kotel Maaravi,* the Western Wall. This wall has stood for generations, as a symbol of the great tragedy of the Jewish people, the destruction of Jewish independence and of the Temple, but also as a promise of the future return of the Jewish people to its land.

After the War of Independence in 1948, the Armistice Agreement with Jordan, arranged with the help of the United Na-

ions, stipulated that Jews should have free access to their holy
places in the Old City. The agreement was not kept—no matter
what we did, no matter how we urged the United Nations to get
Jordan to comply with its terms.

For over nineteen years no Jew could go to what is called the
Wailing Wall. Last Friday morning, I once more went into the
Old City. The military governor, Hayim Herzog, told me of
the valor of the paratroopers; they were the first ones to come
into the Old City, fighting for every inch of it. The commander
of the paratroopers, a tough fighter—he had been in all the battles that had to be fought—wept when he spoke of his men.
When he would get in touch with groups in the various parts of
the city and ask about casualties, the men in command would
answer, "Never mind about the casualties. We are going forward."

Then I went to the Wailing Wall. How I regret my inability
to express either in writing or speech even a small part of what
happened during those few minutes while I was there early that
morning. A number of the paratroopers were very pious, with
tzitzas hanging out from under the jackets of their uniforms.
They placed their Sten guns on a table nearby, put on *tvillen*
and *talasim,* and after first kissing the stones of the wall, they
wept. But it was not a wailing wall anymore. These were not
Jews who had come to the wall to wail because they were not
free and because we had not yet come home. These were men
who had fought a bitter battle and who believed that this wall
was now a symbol of the future and of the independence and
dignity of Israel.

These men who had seen their comrades fall near them in
battle knew that, due to their sacrifice, they stood at last, in front
of the Wailing Wall, weeping, but not wailing in sorrow, offering a prayer of thanksgiving that we were here again, free Israelis in the city of Jerusalem.

All fair men in the world, particularly those that have influence on international affairs, should in this hour ask themselves
this question: Should Israel be urged to withdraw, and if urged,
should Israel comply with the request? Consider our situation.

Here we are. We're a wonderful people, they tell us. We win wars though few against many. Boys fall. Many of those that fought in the War of Independence fell. Their younger brothers went to war ten years ago. The younger brothers of those that fought ten years ago went to war only last week.

There are some mothers who lost sons in all the three wars, but they are wonderful people—these Israelis. Look what they can achieve against such odds. Now that they have won this battle, let them go back where they came from so that the hills of Syria will again be open for Syrian guns, so that Jordanian Legionaires, who shoot and shell at will, can again stand on the towers of the Old City of Jerusalem; so that the Gaza Strip will again become a place from which infiltrees are sent to kill and ambush.

Is there anybody who has the boldness to say to the Israelis: "Go home! Begin to prepare your nine- and ten-year-olds for the next war, perhaps in ten years." You say, "No." I am sure that every fair person in the world in power and out of power, will say, "No," and forgive me for my impudence, more important than all—the Israelis say, "NO!"

I want to describe to you briefly the spirit of our people. One Israeli family that left Israel about a half a year ago, due to economic difficulties, returned with their children just a week before the war broke out. At the airport, the father was asked, "Why did you come back now?" He answered, "I had to return to live in peace!" And that was true.

If you went through the streets of Tel Aviv and Jerusalem and Haifa and Beersheba, or through the settlements, during those weeks of tension, you would see no sign of panic. No mother, no grandmother tried to keep her son or grandson back. Everybody was mobilized. In one place when the reserves came up and reported, there was disorder. One hundred and ten percent of the reserves had reported; hence, there was trouble. Everybody wanted to be in it, to have a share in the struggle.

Now the war on the battlefield is over; the battle in the United Nations has begun. On your television, on your radio, you hear falsehood and evil distortion. One would imagine that we were 40,000,000 who had attacked a poor little nation of 2,000,000. We are called criminals! Nazis! What crime have we committed? We won the war!

While this new battle is getting under way, we must immediately begin to rebuild everything that was destroyed in the Old City, in the northern settlements, in the south, in the houses of the New City of Jerusalem—wherever the shells struck. I am sure that pretty soon we will hear that Jerusalem is a holy city for all religions. Yet when Jerusalem was shelled in 1948, nobody defended Jerusalem, the holy city of all religions! The only people who defended Jerusalem and its sanctuaries at that time were the Jews.

The same took place now, when Jerusalem was shelled. Our boys recaptured Jerusalem fighting hand to hand in the narrow streets, suffering heavy casualties so as not to demolish the ancient holy places with mortars. But we must begin to rebuild. We have much to do for those who are in Israel now and for the many who will come. We must do it together with you, for everything that we have done in Israel until now, we have done together.

During the fighting and the week before the fighting, young Jews from all over the world were trying to reach Israel. At the London airport there were riots because El Al, the only airline flying to Israel during the war, could not possibly take all those that wanted to come. Therefore, I ask the youth of America, if you came in war, why not in peace? The settlements must be reconstructed. In Gadot not one building remains. In all the settlements on the Syrian border much work has to be done as well as in the other settlements along the borders. We want more strength, not only in arms—but in people in the settlements, in the schools, in the universities, in the cities. You are filled with joy because we have remained alive. You want us to be safe in the future, too. Can we not work close together rather than at long distance? Can we not build together in Ein Gev, in Tel Katzir, in Jerusalem, and in Tel Aviv?

And so Israel goes on—in peace, we hope. But nobody can be mistaken any longer. This nation, this Jewish people, this state of Israel, has exactly the same right of self-defense as any other people in the world—no more but no less. We pray that we will never again have to send our sons into battle. We pray that our Arab neighbors will finally realize that peace is as necessary for them as for us. This is our hope.

18. The Zionist Purpose

A statement by Mrs. Meir at Dropsie College. (In English, November 26, 1967)

In this place of learning I shall venture to indulge in some thoughts as to what this is all about; by "this" I mean Israel. I think many people in the world—many Jews and certainly non-Jews—wonder at times why there is so much ado about so little a place: little in area, little in population, tucked away in a far part of the earth among large neighbors in a place that connects great continents—and a place too often in the headlines.

I will not go into current history—at any rate, not very much. But as I look back I want to consider the question of what the Jewish pioneers of the last three generations were trying to accomplish. What was the mission they thought was placed on them to execute?

In the first place, these were people—whether we speak of the BILU * in the eighties of the last century or of the Second Aliyah†—who believed that the Jewish people had existed throughout the ages through a specific (probably peculiar) desire to live rather than to perish. This persistent longing was perhaps contrary to all that one would have expected. A people

* First modern pioneering movement of Zionists.
† Second immigration wave to Palestine, 1904 to end of World War I.

scattered in all corners of the world twice in its history, living as a minority among majorities of different cultures, different religions, different ways of life, and yet remaining a people, was certainly peculiar.

I am now not referring to pogroms, massacres, and major discrimination. I only refer to the accepted disadvantages that Jews have enjoyed, even when at various times in our history Jews lived among people who were not anti-Semitic, where they did not know pogroms, where they were not humiliated as they were in czarist Russia and other places. But even in comparatively favorable circumstances they were a minority: Their religion was different; their day of rest was different. From the beginning the books their children read were as a rule in a different language. Yet, despite all handicaps, whether wholly evil or negatively good, here we are.

One asks: How? In my mind there is no doubt that religion, not only general religious concepts but minute and detailed observances, contributed to this endurance. Even those of us who do not observe the rules incumbent upon a pious Jew must in all objectivity conclude that religious observance has been a major factor in the oneness of the Jewish people. We have seen this to be true in Israel in a dramatic manner, especially after the establishment of the state when people came to us from the caves of Libya and the hills of Morocco and Yemen. When one saw these immigrants together with European Jews and Israeli-born youngsters, one had to ask himself: What did these various people have in common? Not language; certainly not a way of life; certainly not standards of education; certainly not adjustment to the technology and science of our age.

We had nothing in common except one thing: All of us were Jews. I'll never forget a meeting with a little Yemenite boy of twelve after the mass immigration from Yemen. I saw him in one of the newly established villages where Yemenites had been settled, and I asked him how long he had been here. He said, "Only a few weeks." I asked him how long he had been in Israel, and he told me, "Close to a year." And he used very good Hebrew. So I asked him how he knew Hebrew. He looked at me with disdain and said: *Ani yodea torah—ivrit m'hatorah!* ("I know Torah—Hebrew comes from the Torah.") Every boy and man that came from Yemen knew how to read because he read his Bible. (No girl or woman knew how to read or write because women did not have to know the Bible.) Yemen was far away. We didn't know the Yemenites; they didn't know us, but the bond between us existed.

The BILU and the people of the Second Aliyah were very conscious of the continuity of the Jewish people, of the oneness of the Jewish people. I believe that their interpretation of the concept of *ato b'chartonu* ("You have chosen us") meant not that we were chosen as better than other people, nor were we chosen—as some have wished to interpret it, including many Jews—to be dispersed among the peoples in order to teach them moral concepts and other virtues. Our pioneers interpreted *ato b'chartonu* to mean that when Jews would return to their homeland, and when they alone would be responsible for their home and society, they would make a better society. This is my explanation for their absolute devotion to the concept of Jewish peoplehood and the reestablishment of Jewish independence, combined at the same time with an equal fervor for the nature of the society which would emerge in this independent Jewish state: their desire that it should be something better than what had been known in most parts of the world. These pioneers believed that neither a social nor a national ideal was alien to Jewish thought, Jewish religion, or the vision of our prophets. Both had to be realized.

Still another significant element marked their attitude. In my forty-six years in Israel I have not known a man or woman in this group who thought of himself as a "giver" to the country or to the people or who felt that he had sacrificed himself. In Israel, we are much less sentimental and emotional outwardly than we really are within. You probably know that Israeli-born children are called sabras ("prickly pears") because on the outside they are very prickly. Only later did we learn how juicy and sweet they were within. But one usually sees the prickly exterior. Among ourselves we do not usually indulge in long discussions or analyses about why we came and what we did. But if we started probing, we would find that nobody considered that he had done something for someone else; rather that he viewed himself as a "chosen" one or one of the "chosen" generation because he was enabled to do what he did. Generations of Jews throughout the ages had really sacrificed themselves—up to the giving of their lives—for their religion, for their Jewishness, and had accomplished only the strengthening of the obstinacy to carry on among those who were left. At last came generations equally ready for every trial, but who through their endeavor not only endured but accomplished and built for the people. This achievement was granted only to these new generations.

Let me illustrate what I am trying to say by describing three or four types of men and women who came to the land, who achieved something and were responsible for their achievement. Who is more responsible: he who had the idea or those who accept the idea and put life into it? The men of whom I think belonged to both groups.

Aaron David Gordon, for instance, came to Palestine not as a young man; he was not a farmer. He was a Zionist in the sense that he believed that Israel had to be reestablished, that it could be done, and that he had to take part in the process, but on one condition: that the building and the reestablishment of the country be done by those who came, not by others. He believed that the Jewish social order to emerge in Palestine should be better than the societies of the contemporary world. But he did not believe in preaching to others. His philosophy held that everyone must live his life so as to influence those about him by example. In 1905, he did not go to a part of Palestine that was already populated or reclaimed; he was among the first who went out to Deganiah.*

What did Deganiah represent in those days? The settlement was on the other side of the Jordan, in a swampy, deserted section of the country in Lower Galilee, where there were no

---

* "Mother of Kvutzot," pioneer kibbutz, founded in 1908.

Jewish settlers. The few Arab villages in the vicinity were less than friendly. Yet that abandoned locality was the one that Gordon and his friends chose. And how did they go there? Each one individually? They went as a group. These first nine men and women went as a collective group based on a simple principle—which in spite of its simplicity is so difficult to carry out—namely, from each according to his ability, to each according to his need. Incidentally, this was years before the collectives in Russia; up to this day there is no similarity whatever between the voluntary kibbutz and the enforced collective farm of the Soviet state.

Moving stories have been told and written about the difficulties and the tragedies of this lonely kibbutz—difficulties due to the climate, hostile Arabs, the swamps, malaria, and the fact that most of the settlers had never seen a real farm. When the first child was born, its mother took care of it. But when a second child was born, to another mother, a new problem arose. Should each mother stay home and take care of her child? How would this affect the work of the group? How would the women do their share in the building of the economy? The first mother that went out to work and left her child in the care of another mother constituted a revolution.

Forms of kibbutzim vary, and there have been many developments in their structure since then, but basically all the kibbutzim in Israel are established on the same principle—that of cooperative labor. As a member of the kibbutz, Gordon never missed a day of work. This is how his example and that of his group influenced the whole country.

Let me mention another completely different type: Berl Katzenelson, the spiritual giant of Israel's labor movement, a man who asked himself many questions before he gave an answer and who was never ashamed to admit that he was wrong and to start something else. He came to Palestine in 1906, to the kibbutz of Kinnereth, after he had become disillusioned about other attempted solutions of the Jewish problem. He no longer hoped that a revolution in Russia would, in its wake, solve the Jewish problem. He had taken part in the revolutionary movement and decided on the basis of his experience that hope lay elsewhere. He went to Palestine after considering all the difficulties posed by the Arabs and the Turkish regime. He had been earlier attracted by Territorialism.* Many of you know that we were offered Uganda.† (When several years ago I visited Uganda on an official mission, I was happy that we were not there: not because Uganda isn't beautiful but because I couldn't see myself explaining to the local people what Jews were doing there.) Though Katzenelson had been deeply involved in the Russian revolutionary movement and in Territorialism, he was still a young man when he came to Palestine. He had decided that the only meaningful solution for the Jews was to be found in the reestablishment of Jewish independence in Palestine—and in no other place. A Jewish society would have to arise there on a foundation of moral principles, of justice, and of human dignity. He brought up two generations of young people in this light.

A brilliant journalist, a brilliant speaker—not an orator—he would never speak at his audience. One always had a feeling that he was discussing something with his audience. Above all, he was an educator. I don't think he would have forgiven us if in his presence we had called him a "leader." That concept was foreign to him, as I hope it is foreign to us even today. He was one of us. He could walk for hours if he knew that somewhere there was a young person with whom it was worthwhile to discuss and think. He was a man—like many of his colleagues—who did not think it particularly courageous to attack political enemies, but thought it much more important to criticize, severely if necessary, his own party and his own organization.

Together with Ben-Gurion and others, he was among the founders of the Histadrut, a labor federation unique as a trade union. It had to be. When it was organized in 1920, there were

* A movement at the turn of the century dedicated to finding any proper territory for Jewish self-determination.

† Actually it was an area in Kenya offered officially to the Zionist organization by the British Colonial Secretary, Joseph Chamberlain. It became popularly known as the Uganda Plan. It was rejected by the Zionists.

4,000 Jewish workers in the entire country. A big debate was precipitated by a small group who wanted the "class struggle" to be the main paragraph in the constitution of Histadrut at a time when there was not even a class against whom to struggle —neither a working class nor a capitalist class. The only struggle that had to be waged was against the swamps and deserts and rocks. And against the settlers' ignorance of physical labor. They were not farmers; they were not masons; they were not road builders. This was the struggle. It required a lot of courage on the part of Katzenelson and Ben Zvi and Ben-Gurion, who were committed Socialists, to realize that the situation in Palestine did not lend itself to dogmatic answers, that we could not with closed eyes passively follow labor movements in other countries and do exactly as they did.

For us it was not a question of fighting against bad conditions or for more favorable economic conditions. First something had to be built. So Histadrut became not only a labor movement, but an organization which to a very large extent was responsible for the fact that, in 1948, there already was an economy in the country, that there were factories, and that there were Jews who knew how to work together. Because there were no capitalists, the Histadrut had to become its own employer and its own investor.

All this was quite different from the practice of other trade union movements in the world. Above all, Histadrut treasured the dignity of the individual. Without the individual nothing could be done; his devotion and his discipline were essential. But the individual was not a tool for something. He was the maker of tools. He was the one who must build. Even for the best purpose it is criminal to turn an individual into simply a means for some ultimate end. A society in which the dignity of the individual is destroyed cannot hope to be a decent society.

Another man, whose name very few in this audience have probably heard, was Shmuel Yavnieli. He came from Eastern Europe like most of the others. Imbued with a labor philosophy, a scholar and a writer, he too became a pioneer. By that time— 1908–09—word of the remote Yemenite Jews, almost a lost tribe, had reached Palestine. Yavnieli took it upon himself, after discussions with his colleagues, to bring the great message of the return to Zion to the Jews of Yemen. It was an almost impossible task for a Jew to enter Yemen. By donkey Yavnieli traveled rocky paths and mountain roads for months bringing his tidings. And the Jews in Yemen received him almost like the Messiah, for he came from Jerusalem. He told them of the miracles of rebirth happening in Zion, assuring them: "I have come to tell you that soon our land will be free. Every part of the land of Israel that is worked by Jewish hands is liberated."

The first emigration of Jews from Yemen did not take place after the establishment of the state, as it is generally believed; it took place forty years earlier in the days of Yavnieli. And I must say that Israel would have been a poorer place if we had not had the tribe of Yemen with us throughout the years. When the Yemenites reached Palestine, they realized that Yavnieli was not the Messiah, but they never forgot that he had done something messianic.

I want to mention a woman, too: Rachel Blaustein, a young, delicate girl from Russia who came to Palestine at the beginning of the twentieth century. A poet, she came to work on the soil in a new settlement near the Sea of Galilee. Some of her most beautiful poems were written about her work in the fields, though the labor was far beyond her physical capabilities. Throughout her short life, she grieved because she could not do physical work.

The idea that one must work with his hands was common to all. Some people criticize us even today for supposedly not having enough appreciation for the toil of the mind, the toil of the spirit. However, Jews, wherever they were, always busied themselves with the things of the mind and studied if only given the chance. What was lacking in Jewish life were Jews who could work with their hands.

When I was in the Foreign Office of Israel, I went on an official visit to Mexico. At a dinner, my host, the Foreign Minister of Mexico, said to me: "I must ask you something. What has happened to your people? You have never been known as farmers. How have you become excellent farmers? Even in Mexico a group of your men is now teaching some of our people various phases of agriculture."

It is easy to explain, but perhaps easy things are difficult to understand. The explanation lies in our history. For centuries the soil was taboo for Jews, especially in Eastern Europe. We could not own land, we could not work in the fields. We were pushed into the ghettos of a few cities. That was the historical background for our insistence on agricultural work. Men and women among the first to come to Palestine—the BILU, the First Aliyah, the Second Aliyah, and the Third Aliyah—understood the basic need for our social reconstruction. Had they not, we would never have won independence.

And I believe that if we had not understood this necessity, we would not have merited independence. It would have been too easy for a small number of Jews to come to Palestine, to buy orange groves and let Arabs work them. Arab labor was easier to get along with than Jewish labor. It was cheaper. Arabs had no fancy ideas about an eight-hour day. In many ways it would have been simpler to have Arab workers and Jewish landlords. But if this had been the turn of events, there would have been no room for Jews and no right for us to return to a land reclaimed through the toil of others. The pioneer settlers saved the Jewish people and the opportunity for the reestablishment of Jewish independence, because a simple, but basic principle became their bible: It was called *avodah atzmit*—self-labor.

Jews had to teach themselves to work with their hands. The Third Aliyah with its special Hashomer Hatzair group consisted of boys and girls who usually came from the homes of merchants, rabbis, scholars; many were from prosperous assimilated families. Yet they were the ones who built the first road between Tiberias and Nazareth. Labor was their creed. That was the faith each had to accept if he really wanted to build the country. We had to build it. The houses had to be built by us. The roads had to be built by us. The wheat had to be raised by us. The swamps had to be drained by us. This gave us a moral right to the land in addition to the historic right.

If there are no more swamps in Palestine, it is because we drained them. If there are forests, it is because we planted the seedlings. If there are fewer deserts, it is because our children went to the arid areas and reclaimed them.

A word or two about another question that my colleague in Mexico posed. It was after the Suez campaign, in 1956, and he asked: "You were never known as experts in the military field. What happened?" I wonder what he would have asked now, after the Six-Day War. After I tried to explain why we had become good farmers, I could only tell him that we had been obliged to become good soldiers. But not with joy. We are good farmers with joy. It's a wonderful thing to go down to a kibbutz deep in the Negev and remember what it was twenty-five years ago: sand and sky; maybe a well of brackish water. To go down there now and realize that there is practically no fruit that does not grow there, to see orchards and fields, green and lovely, fills the heart with joy. To be good soldiers is our extreme necessity, but there is no joy in it.

We had to learn lessons from history. We are not the only nation whose fate it was to have its country occupied by foreign powers at some time. But in most instances the people remained in the land; they could at some time revolt, throw out the foreign power, and regain independence. Such a situation means fighting, loss of life, and suffering, but the basis for renewal remains. To us, fate was not so kind. Twice in our history, before the state of Israel was reborn, our independence was destroyed by foreign powers who not only occupied the country and put us under their rule; we were twice dispersed and scattered to all corners of the earth.

If our youngsters fight well, it is because they know both ancient and recent history. They know that the Arab powers who declared war the third time in twenty years had in mind for us exactly the same fate as that suffered by the Jews of Old Jerusalem when it was conquered by the Jordanian Army in 1948 or the fate of the kibbutzim in Kfar Etzion. Nobody was left to live in peace. Destruction was the fate that awaited us— in '48, in '56, in '67, not the prospect of a foreign occupation.

That the Jewish people survived the two ancient dispersions in our history is something at which the world has marveled. Were the third chance history has offered lost, a fourth chance might perhaps never come.

Let us not forget that the state of Israel was established after 6,000,000 Jews in Europe had perished. They were the natural reservoir of our religion, of Zionism, of Jewish culture, and of Hebrew culture. With that reservoir gone, with 3,000,000 Jews shut behind the iron curtain, with millions of Jews in the free world who, in addition to enjoying authentic freedom, are free to assimilate, free not to know Hebrew, free not to go to the synagogue, free not to know the Bible, free from kinship with the Jewish people, the fear under which we live is that if Israel is annihilated, that fateful historic opportunity will be lost forever.

Several months before that terrible black day when your President was assassinated, I had the great privilege of speaking to him on a security problem in Israel. At one point I said to him: "Mr. President, the government of Israel, like every other decent government, worries about the welfare of its people and the security of the country. In that, we are no different from other states. But we have an extra responsibility which probably no other government has: that is our long memory of what happened to us twice in the past, and our fear that we may be remembered as the generation which after the annihilation of 6,000,000 Jews had an opportunity to reestablish Jewish sovereignty and did not know how to hold it. This fear to face history is something additional."

And I had no doubt in my mind that when President Kennedy said, "I understand," he understood.

Maybe this is the second reason why we are good soldiers. We are good farmers because anything built on any other foundation except our own hard physical work would never have prospered. In addition, we are conscious of our responsibility to history; as you go through Israel, you cannot help being conscious of history. This is what the present-day Israeli feels. He must protect the future not only for himself and his family, not only for those who are in Israel, today, but for those who could not come and for those who will come.

We are driven by the memory of the past, the responsibility for the future, and by the desire to live up to a sense of "chosenness"—not because we are better than others, but because we dream of doing better in building a society in Israel which will be a good society founded on concepts of justice and equality.

19. "We Are Rooted in This Soil"

A statement made on the occasion of Mrs. Meir's receiving an honorary degree of Humane Letters from the Hebrew Union College Biblical and Archaeological School of Jerusalem. (In Hebrew, October 13, 1970)

Each one of us, as he studies the history of our people, ponders from time to time on what the Jewish people might have been had Jews acted differently than they did at a particular time or place. Often we are simply unable to explain in a rational way how the great miracle occurred which made us what we are today.

We are an ancient people, and we speak of thousands of years as if they were but days or weeks. Just a few weeks ago we celebrated the nineteen hundredth anniversary of the destruction of the Second Temple. Nineteen hundred years, and still Jewry survives, scattered in all corners of the earth! I am not referring to Jews who were unable to fulfill their destiny or to survive physically in the face of pogroms or persecutions. I refer to Jews whose heroism enabled them to remain Jewish in a spiritual national sense. Often we lament the divisiveness which exists within the Jewish people, and we speak (too often, in my opinion) in an exaggerated way about our failings and shortcomings. Yet we possess this remarkable capacity of remaining a united people despite the many differences which persist among us. We are indeed, if I may be permitted to say so, the most nonconformist of peoples—at least we are non-conformist in our relationship to each other. Each of us is impelled to express himself with great individual emphasis and firmness, yet despite it all, our unity as a people remains strong after the lapse of so many centuries and in the direst circumstances.

As I watch this important institution of higher learning, the Hebrew Union College Biblical and Archaeological School of Jerusalem, develop in our midst and, above all, see this group of young men from the Hebrew Union College-Jewish Institute of Religion in America who came here for at least a year, I cannot help but wonder what would happen if I were to take each one of them aside and ask him who he is and from where he came. How many generations has his family lived in America? Has the Jewish bond which ties him to the past generations never been severed? Has Jewish education always been successful? I have no doubt that we would discover that the tie was cut at one time or another, and yet these young men are with us.

In this connection I cannot help but recall another Jewish community. Last night, or rather early this morning, I sat at my desk and read tens of letters signed by tens of Soviet Jews. Some were written by groups and some by individuals. All of them expressed one idea with such force that as I read their words, my Zionism and my sense of belonging to this land seemed almost less strong than theirs. And who are they? Middle-aged men in their fifties or elderly men in their sixties and seventies? I read a letter signed by ten Jews, young people born in 1936, 1937, 1940, 1950, expressing their passionate desire to live their lives as Jews in Israel—a letter made public in Russia, regardless of its personal, economic, and political consequences.

In the face of this phenomenon, each of us must ask the question: Whence this miracle? The Russian Jews are living in a spiritual desert, and what a desert it is! Yet they express their will to be with us, to live in Israel. They live amid a gigantic and mighty nation and yet do not belong to it. They declare that their dwelling place is alien to them, that they belong to their own land, to the land of Israel. They do not make this pronouncement secretly or in the underground but address it to the Soviet government and to the world. There is no assurance that they will ever arrive here. What they have done, they did without any illusions as to their safety. They are well schooled in the ways of Soviet society and are well aware of the possible consequences of their writing to us. Yet letter after letter ends on the same note: "I am prepared for anything, but I have one desire, and that is to live and die in Israel." When I see them in my mind's eye and then look at the group of students I have just addressed, how wide is the difference between them! Each is so utterly different from the other, except for this one factor, which cannot be rationally explained.

I remember that in my teens I would often have theological arguments with my mother. I wanted very much to explain to her that everything ultimately came from nature, that there was science and that science has laws. During one of these discussions she won the argument by repeating, "*Nu*, Goldala, let's see you make the rain come." Whenever I see people among us who are educated, clever, and able to explain everything, I ask them whether one does not at the end finally reach the unexplainable, the ultimately unknowable. It really is not important what you call it. Let us assume that for the sake of common agreement we call that something "spirit"—the spirit of this people—which has no limitations and is indestructible. This spiritual strength is eternal. It is transmitted from generation to generation, almost unwittingly. This is the most important factor in our lives. Whatever we do, whatever we believe should be done, springs from this spirit.

I want to thank Dr. Glueck, and the Hebrew Union College, not only because they came here with their students so that they might learn something about our country and our youth. I venture to suggest that this encounter will also be good for our own young people. I am always a little afraid that precisely here, where it is so wholesome and easy to be a Jew, where one can view oneself and his own generation as a natural link to the Jewish past without any need to argue or to prove the point, there lurks a potential danger for the continued strength of our uniqueness. I am sometimes fearful that Jewish consciousness in Israel might become too natural, too unreflective, and that our sabras might lose the sense of wonder at the miracle of Jewish survival. Should this happen, something very basic would be missing from the souls of our young people.

It is therefore good that members of this generation of Israelis meet young Jews like your students, who at first sight might seem to be strangers; but then they discover a unity binding them together beyond the difference of language and circumstances, that the strangers are really close relatives, members of one people. In this way the young Israelis will learn the great reality of our being one people, wherever we may be, united despite all the differences that superficially separate us. Differences in modes of religious expression, I believe, will become less and less important in the future, for beyond them, the decisive factor of the unity of Israel everywhere will prevail.

I want to make one further point. Nelson Glueck has done something wonderful for us. He was not content with the spirit alone. He wanted to prove that the spirit of the Jewish people is rooted in its soil, in the simplest and most physical sense of the word. The Jewish spirit is not something that floats about in a vacuum. Our bond with this land is not only spiritual. Go out and look: Israel is made up of a stone here, a tree there, a road, a hill; study the books Glueck has written about the Jordan Valley and the Negev. In this hall I see his colleague, Professor Yadin, who shares this sense of concreteness, of our physical relationship with the soil and atmosphere of the very land of Israel. They and their fellow archaeologists here dwell on the natural and blessed link between the Jewish spirit and the concrete facts of our history, our rootedness in the soil of this holy land. We are not the people of the spirit in the sense that we hover between heaven and earth. We have earth, and we have sky! Where there is soil there is also spirit. This spirit cannot be shaken because it is deeply rooted in its soil!

I hope that your institution will grow and that you will bring more of your young people here. Let those who go back to America for the time being return here again later, in order to increase the fold of those who will come to live here permanently. Let them help build this nation and this land in the image of what we wish it to be. We are talking today at a comparatively tranquil moment. You should come here, like many other Jews from many different countries, not only in hours of tranquillity, but also during the great storms.

It is possible that our fate still has many difficulties and dangers in store for us. However, just as from my childhood on I have believed firmly in Jewish independence, so I believe in perfect faith that we will live in a Jewish state which will be just, creative, and dedicated to the Jewish spirit. It will be rich in the enduring qualities of our age-old and ever-new tradition, and it will be a Jewish state at peace with our neighbors. Many Jews will come here, as many already have come, not because they have no other choice, but precisely because they are free to choose the Jewish state as the one that is the best, the most beautiful, and the only one for them.

20. An Equal Chance

A plea for equality of opportunity for all peoples made to the Second World Conference of Engineers and Architects, held in Israel. (December 14, 1970)

It is not enough for education to be free and for schools to be accessible to all. We cannot ignore the difference between a child who leaves a home with books and returns after school to a quiet room in which to prepare his lessons and a child with none of these advantages. A child whose father and mother can teach him and help him in his lessons is obviously not in the same situation as a child whose parents had no schooling.

Theoretically, we may provide equal educational opportunity. The school is open on the same terms to the child of a comfortable home as it is to a family of six, eight, and ten children who occupy a tiny flat or house of two or three small rooms, filled mainly by beds. But the inequality of the homes results in a basic inequality which is revealed in what these children accomplish.

How often do we hear failure in school explained by a dismissal of the disadvantaged child: "Well, these children are just not capable." We pass judgment and divide humanity. Nor is this division limited to education. We all remember when the developing countries were thought of as peoples that could not rule themselves; they were simply not capable. Most of us here who belong to the category of developing countries are at most twenty-five years old—some considerably less—and we had to prove our capacity, whatever the conditions.

We in Israel, as all of you in your countries, took the risk of independence. Happy are those who did not have to fight for the privilege of proving that they were capable of being free; some of us did. All of us started with various degrees of disadvantage. And we have all come into a hard world—not a world of peace, in which good-intentioned people with high ideals sit in a conference room, considering the problems before them. The world's spokesmen do not survey the world's wants and generously announce: "These are our resources. Let's see what we can do with them."

Most of us acquired independence after the Second World War. I don't know how many of us cherished illusions that this was the end of all wars. Those of my age who lived through the First World War had such illusions; we were sure that this was the war that ended all wars. I am afraid that the new generation after the Second World War was wiser, almost skeptical, and no sooner was the terrible bloodshed of the great war over than small wars began to erupt round the globe. Since the end of the Second World War we have practically had no peace in the world.

To all the horror that war entails must be added a tragic by-product. Under the strains of war the affluent world cannot do all it should for developing countries. There are more important demands on its funds: instead of tractors, tanks; instead of school buildings, Army camps; instead of hospitals, bombers. And how much skill and planning go into making these instruments more effective from year to year? This plane is not good enough; this bomber is not good enough. It does not kill enough. With what devotion better bombers, more effective bombs are sought. And therefore how much money is left for such simple matters as schools and hospitals and roads and parks and decent housing and food and education?

In a world that longs desperately for peace, we developing countries have a special stake. We have no large ambitions.

None of us is going to conquer empires. None of us requires anything that some other country has. I dare to say that if the developing countries were not to lend themselves to any purpose that does not directly lead to peace, we could achieve one more great thing after the great thing we did when we set ourselves free. We could set the world free. It depends upon us. I am afraid that too many of us consider the big affluent countries solely to blame. Perhaps they are, here and there, but where are we?

You may wonder what all this has to do with architecture and engineering? But what difference does it make how well the city is planned, how beautiful the houses are, how well paved the roads, how wide the streets, when there is the danger of destruction—even well-planned cities have been bombed out in the past. Planning a house, a street, a park, after all, has no value whatever if it does not make for a more productive life, for the child, man, and woman who live in that house.

I know that we have very many bread-and-butter problems in planning and in engineering; I only want to leave one thought with you drawn from my experience. In 1949 I became Minister of Labor. At that time Israel had 200,000 men, women, and children in camps and tents; in many tents there were two families; some of these were the hundreds of thousands of Jews who had remained in Europe alive after the Holocaust and had come from DP camps in Germany and Cyprus; others had come from underdeveloped countries in our area, among them people who had lived in caves.

I remember long discussions about their housing. How do we build for them? You must remember how limited were our means and how unlimited the demands upon them. Hence, the long arguments about economy: "These immigrants are not accustomed to a house with all the amenities. They won't know how to live in a house of this kind. Don't build a bathroom, a shower room; they'll only put all their junk there. They won't know what a shower is." That's true. Many had never seen a shower in the countries from which they came. But I remember one day with great joy. A delegation from a new immigrant village came to me with a serious complaint: Their shower did not have hot running water, only cold water.

Almost instinctively I was impatient. I knew their countries of origin and that they had never seen so much as a bathroom in their lives; they never had a tap of running water in their house. But fortunately I controlled myself, realizing what a wonderful complaint this was. In such a short time these immigrants had learned to want showers, to want not only cold water, but hot water. They were entitled to it. This proves that people do not enjoy living under impossible conditions. Their demands rise with their opportunities.

Most of you do not have the same problems that Israel has. Israel has been obliged to engage in double planning, one for building and one to defend what we have already built. I wish all of you, whether you come from developed or developing countries, peace, for the entire world, so that all of us together may make one world where every human being has an equal chance, a world that is one in joy and in building.

21. Israel's Search for Peace

An extensive survey of Israel's political and security position given by the Prime Minister to the Knesset. (In Hebrew, May 26, 1970)

At the opening of our parliamentary session, I wish to survey the security and political conjuncture. In recent months, and in the past weeks especially, the security situation has worsened seriously on the southern front in particular, and the harmful effect of that is felt on the other fronts also.

The main feature of this escalation and tension is an advanced and dangerous stage of Soviet involvement in Egypt, at the beck and call of Egyptian aggression and infractions of the cease-fire. There is no precedent for this involvement in the history of Soviet penetration into the Middle East; it is encouraging Egypt in its plan to renew the war of attrition and so move further along the path of its mounting ambition to vanquish Israel.

To understand the background, we must recall Nasser's declared decision, in the spring of 1969, to abrogate the cease-fire and ignore the cease-fire lines. It is typical of Egyptian policy all along its warmongering way. It reflects a basic doctrine—that Israel is an exception in the family of nations: The rules that civilized countries accept do not apply to Israel; an international obligation toward Israel is to be undertaken only if there is no other option, no possible alternative, and it may be renounced at the first chance. Routed on the battlefield, you

184

acquiesce in international proposals and arrangements that enable you to rescue your regime. But should it appear that your military strength has been sufficiently restored to let you attack, you may treat your undertaking or your signature as though it had never been. Such was the end of Egypt's cease-fire undertaking of 9 June, 1967, entered into at the instance of the Security Council. Such was the end of Egypt's earlier regional and international undertaking on matters concerning Egypt and Israel. This behavior illuminates the intentions and credibility of Cairo in all that governs its attitude toward peace with Israel.

Egypt ignored its own signature of the Armistice Agreement of 1949. In the eyes of its rulers, the agreement was no more than a temporary device to save Egypt from total collapse after its abortive aggression and afford it a breathing space to prepare for a new campaign. Within a few years, Egypt—characteristically disavowing its international pledges—had flouted the Security Council and jettisoned the principle of freedom of navigation. With Nasser's accession to power, the Egyptians wholly emptied the Armistice Agreement of its content by regularly dispatching bands of murderers from the Gaza Strip into Israel.

Nasser next started to subvert those Arab regimes of which he did not approve and which would not bow to his authority. He opened up the Middle East to Soviet penetration, he launched a plan to form a unified military command of the Arab states bordering Israel and pressed forward with feverish preparations for a renewed assault upon us.

In 1956, his second armed threat to our existence was flung back. Once more, he evinced an interest in mediation and international settlement to engineer a withdrawal of Israel's forces from Sinai and, after that, from Sharm el-Sheikh and the Gaza Strip. With his knowledge and concurrence, the United Nations Emergency Force was deployed to ensure freedom of navigation in the Gulf of Aqaba and as a guarantee that the strip would no longer serve as a base for death-dealing incursions into Israel.

For ten years, no plaint was heard from Cairo about the Emergency Force and its functions. But Nasser was engaged all that time—with Soviet help—in building up his Army anew and in subversive and adventurous activity throughout the region, culminating in the bloody war that he fought, unsuccessfully, against the Yemenite people for five years on end.

In 1967, convinced, it seems, that he had the strength to overcome Israel in battle, he disavowed his international commitments wholesale, expelled the Emergency Force, concentrated most of his troops in eastern Sinai, reinstated his blockade of the Straits of Tiran, and prepared for a war of annihilation against Israel—a war which, in his own words, would turn back the clock to before 1948.

Up to 5 June, 1967, he was entirely deaf to the universal appeal to refrain from plunging the Middle East into a third maelstrom of blood and suffering. Four days later, his Army undone, he was not slow to answer the Security Council's call for a cease-fire and so, again, manage to avert calamity for Egypt. The Council's cease-fire resolution was not limited in time or condition. Neither did Nasser attach any limitation of time or other term to his assent.

Proof of his real designs is abundant in his subsequent declarations and deeds. The Khartoum doctrine is unchanged: no peace, no recognition, no negotiation. Israel must withdraw to the borders of 4 June, 1967, and thereafter surrender its sovereignty to the "Palestinian people." Only with that twofold stipulation would the cease-fire be observed by Egypt. The logic is sound: If the stipulations are kept, Nasser's aim is won, and there will be no further cause for him to pursue aggression.

Nasser will not admit the concept of peace in its literal, humane, and Jewish sense. By our definition, and in international consciousness and morality, peace means good neighborliness and cooperation between nations. According to his thinking, to invite Egypt to make peace with Israel is to invite Egypt to accept capitulation and indignity. That is the source of the flood of destruction, anguish, and blood in which the peoples of the Middle East have been drowning, decade after decade.

On 17 March, 1969, when Egyptian artillery began to bombard our soldiers in the Canal Zone, I announced, in this House: "The Arab states must realize that there can be quiet on the cease-fire line only if there is quiet on both sides of it, and not just on one. We want quiet; we want the cease-fire upheld. But this depends on the Arab states. The maintenance of quiet must be reciprocal."

Egypt did not hearken to my words. Its aggressiveness redoubled. At the beginning of May, Nasser told his people that his forces had destroyed 60 percent of the line of fortifications which Israel had built along the Canal, and would keep on until they had demolished what was left. In the ensuing years, not only have our entrenchments been reinforced, but we have hit hard at the Egyptian emplacements and foiled more than one attempt to raid across the Canal.

What Nasser describes as "a war of attrition" began in March, 1969. On 30 March, he could say: "The time has passed when we required any soldier at the front who opened fire on the enemy to account for his action, because we wanted to avoid complications. Now the picture is different: If a soldier at the front sees the enemy and does not open fire, he must answer for it."

In December, 1969, he confirmed his preparedness for war or, in his own phrase, "the advance of the Egyptian Army through rivers of blood and fire."

The Israel Defense Forces have punished this vainglorious aggression. I shall not retell the tale of their courage and resource: the digging in, the daring operations of the Air Force, the power of our armor. Aggression has been repelled, the enemy's timetable upset, and the pressure on our front line eased by our striking at vital enemy targets along the Canal and far behind it, so confounding his plans for all-out war. True, to our great sorrow, we have suffered losses in killed and wounded, but our vigorous self-defense has thwarted Egypt's schemes and its endeavors to wear us down and shake our southern front.

Thus bankrupt, the Cairo regime had only the choice between accepting Israel's constant call to return to reciprocal observance of the cease-fire, as a stepping-stone to peace, or leaning more heavily still on the Soviet Union to the point of asking it to become operationally involved, so that Egypt might carry on the war of attrition, notwithstanding the unpleasant repercussions of that involvement. Egypt chose the second course.

In many of his speeches, Nasser claims credit for ending British power and Egypt's subjugation to it. But the same leader who promised his people full independence from any foreign power has preferred to renew its dependence and subservience rather than make peace with Israel and honor the cease-fire. In his plight, he elects to conceal from his people the truth that, in place of the British, the Soviets are invading the area. This is the pass to which blindness and hatred have brought the Egyptian revolution.

Soviet penetration did not start yesterday or the day before. Its beginning could be seen in the mid-fifties, in a strengthening of influence by the provision of economic aid and weaponry on the easiest terms.

In May, 1967, the Soviet Union provocatively spawned baseless rumors of Israeli concentrations on the Syrian border. This was a major link in the chain of developments that led to the Six-Day War. When the fighting was over, Moscow displayed no readiness to counsel the Arabs to close the chapter of violence and open one of regional cooperation—although, to extricate Nasser, it had voted for the unconditional cease-fire resolution.

In his speech of 1 May, 1970, Nasser confessed that, only three days after Egypt had submitted to that resolution, the Soviets agreed to rearm his forces. He said:

> On 12 June—and now I can reveal it—I received a note from Brezhnev, Kosygin, and Podgorny, in which they promised to support the Arab nation and restore Egypt's armed forces, without any payment, to their prewar level.
>
> Thus we were able to withstand and overcome our plight and rehabilitate our armed forces anew.

Within the past three years, the Soviet Union has supplied Egypt, Syria, and Iraq with 2,000 tanks and 800 fighter aircraft, besides other military equipment, to an overall value of some $3.5 billion, two-thirds to Egypt alone. This armament was purveyed with practically no monetary requital. Thousands of Soviet specialists are engaged in training the Egyptian forces. Soviet advisers are guiding and instructing the Egyptian forces within units and bases even during combat.

It is hard to believe that Nasser would have dared to resume aggression in March, 1969, on a large scale without Russian authorization. It is harder to believe that, in May–June, 1969, he would have abrogated the cease-fire without it. Not only did the Soviet Union not use its influence to urge him to comply with the cease-fire; it even encouraged him to step up his belligerency. A conspicuous example of this disinclination to make its contribution to the restoration of quiet was Moscow's rejection of the American proposal, in mid-February, 1970, for a joint appeal by the four powers to the parties in the region to respect the cease-fire.

It is widely assumed that the Soviet Union is not anxious for an all-out war, in which its protégé, Egypt, would be worsted in battle again, but that, at the same time, it eschews a cease-fire as a stage in progress toward peace. Russia prefers something in between—frontier clashes, indecisive engagements, ongoing tensions, which would allow it to exploit Egyptian dependence to the hilt, and so further its regional pressure on Israel—it seeks to satisfy Egypt's needs in a manner that will not entail the danger of another Egyptian reverse or of a "needless" peace.

Not content with bolstering Nasser's policy of aggression and war, the Soviet Union has embarked upon a campaign of anti-Semitic propaganda within its own borders and of venomous vilification of Israel through all its communication media and in international forums. The Soviets have gone so far in slander as to label us Nazis; without shame or compunction, they charge Jews with taking part in pogroms organized by the czarist regime and of collaborating with the Nazis. They represent Trotsky as a "Zionist." They conduct "scientific" research which has "discovered" that there is no such thing as a Jewish people.

The purpose is twofold: to intimidate Soviet Jewry and to prepare the psychological ground for any and every mischief against Israel.

The failure of the war of attrition and Nasser's pleas have persuaded the Soviets to extend their involvement. At the moment when, in New York and Washington, their representatives were meeting representatives of the Western powers to discuss a renewal of the Jarring mission and a peace settlement, Soviet ships were sailing to Egypt, laden with SA-3 ground-to-air missiles, and thousands of Soviet experts were arriving to install, man, and operate the batteries. In December, 1969, signs of the entrenched bases of ground-to-air missiles could be discerned in the Canal and other zones. We estimate that there are already about twenty such bases in the heart of Egypt.

In mid-April, Soviet involvement went one step further—and the gravest so far. Soviet pilots, from bases at their disposal on Egyptian soil, began to carry out operational missions over wide areas. With that defensive coverage of their rear, the Egyptians could mount their artillery bombardment in the Canal Zone on a scale unparalleled since it was started in March, 1969.

Speaking on 1 May on the intensification of the war against Israel, Nasser told his audience: "In the last fifteen days a change has taken place. As we can see, our forces are taking the initiative in operations." And in the same speech: "All this is due to the aid which the Soviet Union has furnished, and it is clear that you have heard many rumors and are destined to hear many more."

On 20 May, Nasser admitted for the first time, in an interview for the German newspaper *Die Welt,* that Soviet pilots were flying jet planes of the Egyptian Air Force and might clash with ours.

Thus the Middle East is plumbing a new depth of unease. The Soviet Union has forged an explosive link in a chain of acts that is dragging the region into an escalation of deadly warfare and foredooms any hope of peacemaking.

We have informed governments of the ominous significance of this new phase in Soviet involvement. We have explained that a situation has developed which ought to perturb not only Israel, but every state in the free world. The lesson of Czechoslovakia must not be forgotten. If the free world—and particularly the United States, its leader—can pass on to the next item on its agenda without any effort to deter the Soviet Union from selfishly involving itself so largely in a quarrel with which it has no concern, then it is not Israel alone that is imperiled, but no small nation can any longer dwell in safety within its frontiers.

The government of Israel has made it plain, as part of its basic policy to defend the state's being and sovereignty whatever betide, that the Israel Defense Forces will continue to hold the cease-fire line on the southern as on other fronts and not permit it to be sapped or breached. For that purpose, it is essential to stop the deployment of the ground-to-air missile pads which the Egyptians are trying to set up adjacent to the cease-fire line; the protection of our forces entrenched there to prevent the breaching of the front depends on that. No serious person will suspect Israel of wanting to provoke, or being interested in provoking, Soviet pilots integrated into the Egyptian apparatus of war, but neither will anyone in his senses expect us to allow the Egyptian Army to carry through its aggressive plans undeterred. The Israel Defense Forces will use all their strength and skill to defeat these schemes, even if outside factors are helping to carry them out.

All this means that our search for the arms indispensable for our defense has become more urgent, more vital. When we asked to be allowed to buy more aircraft from the United States, we based ourselves on the reality that the balance of power had been shaken by the enormous arsenals provided by the Soviet Union to Egypt free of charge. Since the President of the United States announced deferment of his decision on that critical point, it has, as I have said, become known that SA-3 batteries, with Soviet crews, have been set up in Egypt and Soviet pilots have been activated in operational flights. This adds a new and ominous dimension of imbalance, and the need to redress the equilibrium becomes more pressing and crucial.

We have emphasized to peace-loving governments the necessity to bring their influence to bear and make their protests heard against a Soviet involvement which so dangerously aggravates tension in the Middle East. During his press conference on 8 May, in the light of reports that Soviet pilots had been integrated into Egypt's Air Force, the President of the United States stated that the United States was watching the situation, and if it became clear that the reports were true and the escalation continued, this would drastically shift the balance of power and make it necessary for the United States to reappraise its decision as to the supply of jets to Israel. He also said that the United States had already made it perfectly plain that it was in the interests of peace in the Middle East that no change be permitted in the balance of forces and that the United States would abide by that obligation.

On 24 March of this year, the Secretary of State, in the President's name, declared that the United States would not allow the security of Israel to be jeopardized and that, if steps were taken that might shake the present balance of power or if, in his view, international developments justified it, the President would not hesitate to reconsider the matter.

I do not have to tell you that I attach great importance to these statements. But I must say, with the utmost gravity, that delay in granting our wish hardly rectifies the change for the worse in the balance of power that the new phase in Soviet involvement, with all its attendant perils, has entailed.

There is close and continuous contact between ourselves and the U.S. authorities in the matter. Last week, Foreign Minister Eban had talks with the President and the Secretary of State; he was told that the urgent and detailed survey mentioned by President Nixon four weeks ago was not yet complete, but he was assured that the official United States declarations of 24 March and 8 May on the balance of power held entirely good.

In all our contacts, we have stressed the importance of the time factor, for any lag in meeting our requirements can harm our interests and is likely to be interpreted by our enemies as encouraging their aggression and by the Soviet Union as condoning its intensified involvement. I find it inconceivable that the United States will not carry out its declared undertaking.

Of late, there has been a rise in aggressive activity on the other fronts as well. Nasser is trying to step up the effectiveness of the eastern front, and Egypt's military policy has undoubtedly affected the situation on the other fronts. Its destructive consequences are visible not only in terrorist operations against Israel from Jordan, Syria, and Lebanon, but also in the strategy of neighboring governments and in domestic upheavals in Jordan and Lebanon.

The terrorist organization in Syria is a section of the Syrian Army, acting under government directives. In Jordan and Lebanon, terrorist domination has so expanded as to become a threat to the existence and authority of these governments. In both countries, the governments have vainly sought to reconcile opposites: their own authority and the presence and activity of the terrorist organizations. Such attempts could meet with no more than a semblance of success. More than once, the governments seemed about to confront the organizations but each time recoiled from the encounter.

In Jordan, as in Lebanon, the terrorists have taken heart from Nasser. Through his support, direct and indirect, they have strengthened their position. The authorities have compromised with them at Israel's expense, allowing them no little latitude—against Israel. The terrorists have been accorded a recognized status, which guarantees them freedom of action. The entire world knows of "the Cairo Agreement" between the terrorists and the Lebanese government, achieved through the mediation and under the auspices of Egypt. It allows them to pursue their activities openly, in areas allotted to them, in coordination with the Lebanese authorities and Army, as well as elsewhere along the border.

Between the beginning of January and 20 May, there were

1,100 enemy operations along the Jordanian front. The Fatah and other organizations dug themselves in along the length of the Israel-Lebanon frontier. It has become a focus of murder and sabotage: terrorists were responsible for 140 inroads along that frontier. After a series of such acts, among them Katyusha fire on inoffensive civilians in Kiryat Shmonah and other places, terrorism reached a climax on 22 May in the calculated murder, from ambush, of schoolchildren, teachers, and other passengers in a school bus.

There is no viler example of the vicious mentality and lethal policy of the terrorist organizations and their instructors in the Arab capitals than the developments along the Lebanese front. Until the Six-Day War, it had been the most tranquil of all the frontiers. Even afterward, the tension which marked the cease-fire lines and borders with Egypt and Jordan was absent there, until Fatah and their backers entrenched themselves and decided that the Lebanese border, too, must be set aflame. And there is another aim—common to Cairo and Damascus for a number of years—which has not been wanting in terrorist policy: to prejudice Lebanon's independence and disturb the delicate equipoise between its two religious communities. By accepting the Cairo Agreement in November, 1969, and allowing the establishment of terrorist bases in its territory, Lebanon has been progressively endangering its independence, as Jordan did before.

Endlessly provoked by terrorists from Lebanon, we retaliated a number of times against Fatah bases. The ever closer cooperation between Beirut and the terrorist organizations makes more and more evident the responsibility of the Lebanese government. It cannot be shrugged off. We shall keep on demanding that Beirut use its power to halt aggression from its territory and do its bounden duty in restoring tranquillity.

Israel is interested in the stability of democracy in Lebanon, in its progress, integrity, and peace. On 22 May, Radio Beirut announced that "Lebanon has often stated that it is not prepared on any account to act as a policeman guarding Israel." So long as Lebanon evades its responsibility and allows the terrorists to indulge in aggression and murder, the government of Israel will, by all necessary measures, defend the welfare of Israel's citizens, its highways, towns, and villages.

We must view recent happenings against the whole background of our struggle, since the Six-Day War, to realize Israel's highest aspiration, the aspiration to peace.

To our intense disappointment, we learned on the morrow of the Six-Day War that the rulers of the Arab states and the Soviet Union were not prepared to put an end to the conflict. Witness authoritative declarations by the Arab governments, the resolutions of Khartoum, the Soviet Union's identification with this policy, and its assiduous efforts to rehabilitate the Arab armies with lavish and unstinted aid. We learned that our struggle for peace would be prolonged, full of pain and sacrifice. We decided—and the nation was with us, to a man—resolutely to defend the cease-fire lines against all aggression and simultaneously to press on with our strivings to attain peace.

It is not our way to glorify ourselves, but to render a sober account of our policy, not hiding the hard truth from the people. We and the world know that there is no truth in Egypt's claims of resounding victories. The main efforts of the Egyptian Army have been repelled by the Israel Defense Forces. All claims of success in breaking our line are false. Most attempted sorties by Egyptian planes into our airspace have been thwarted, and the Egyptians pay a heavy price for every venture to clash with our Air Force. We control the area all along the Canal cease-fire line more firmly and strongly than ever.

Soviet involvement has not deterred, and will not deter, Israel from exercising its recognized right to defend the cease-fire lines until secure boundaries are agreed upon within the compass of the peace we so much desire. Had its aggression gained the political objectives set, Egypt could by now have celebrated victory. But Nasser and the Soviets have not realized those aims.

Three years after the Six-Day War, we can affirm that two fundamental principles have become a permanent part of the international consciousness: Israel's right to stand fast on the cease-fire lines, not budging until the conclusion of peace that will fix secure and recognized boundaries, and its right to self-defense and to acquire the equipment essential to defense and deterrence.

I have, on several occasions, explained the differences in appraisal and approach between ourselves and friendly states and powers. I have no intention of claiming that these have entirely disappeared. Nevertheless, we cannot allow them to overshadow the recognition of those twin principles, any more than we may overlook the systematic plotting of our enemies to isolate Israel.

Another front that will test our power to hold out is the economic. How we hold out militarily and politically is contingent on the degree of our success in surmounting economic troubles.

Our victories in three wars, our robust military stance in the interim periods of what, by comparison, has been tranquillity, as well as through these present difficult days, could never have been won without a solidly based economy, a high educational standard of soldier and civilian, a high technological level of worker in every branch. We owe it to an unprecedently rapid economic development and expansion that the national income of tiny Israel almost equals that of Egypt, with a population tenfold ours and more. We must, by all necessary measures, maintain that advantage.

The central problem of the moment arises from an unfavorable balance of payments and the resultant shortage of foreign currency. The deficit in our balance of payments may be attributed, primarily, to the vastly greater defense imports; if those had stayed at their pre-Six-Day-War level, we would by now be nearing economic independence.

Until 1968, capital imports, which pay for any excess of imports over exports, had sufficed not only to cover the deficit, but also to amass considerable reserves of foreign currency. Since then, they are no longer enough. There is a risk of a drop in foreign currency reserves which might prevent our sustaining the level of imports imperative for the smooth working of the economy under conditions of full employment and meeting at the same time our defense requirements.

We must, therefore, in the national interest, make every endeavor and be prepared for every sacrifice demanded for the solving of this problem. Which means that we must also restrict the growth of imports, especially of imports destined for private and public consumption and not for security. The standard of living has risen in the last three years by more than 25 percent; in this period of emergency, our efforts to economize must be mirrored in pegging a standard of living that may have climbed too steeply.

One of the "unavoidables" is to cut down the state budget and saddle the public with taxes, charges, and compulsory loans on no small scale. This action was taken only in the last few weeks, and we hope that it will have the desired and sufficient effect. If it does not, if we find that imports have not been curbed enough or exports not risen enough, that consumption keeps expanding and the deficit swelling, we will not shrink from further action.

Let me add that this implies no change in our determination, even in an emergency that tightens all belts, not to neglect the advancement of the lower-income strata; this year, too, we have adopted a number of significant measures to better their lot, and we shall continue to do so.

The policy is no easy one for those who have to discharge it, nor is it a light burden that it places on the public's shoulders. The understanding and maturity with which the man in the street has accepted these stern dispositions are most commendable; only a negligible minority has tried to circumvent them.

Our economic targets are far from simple of attainment. The ongoing development of the economy, the absorption of new-comers, and enormous defense expenditure present a challenge greater than we could face alone. We are deeply grateful, therefore, for the staunch cooperation of world Jewry and the assistance of friendly nations. I believe that we can continue to rely on that help, but for moral and practical reasons alike, we cannot make demands on others if we do not first do our own share. So we must adjust our way of life, in everything that concerns wages, incomes, consumption, savings, productivity, personal effort, and outlay, each of us playing his full part, to what the overriding national purpose dictates.

The aspiration to peace is not only the central plank in our platform; it is the cornerstone of our pioneering life and labor. Ever since renewal of independence, we have based all our undertakings of settlement and creativity on the fundamental credo that we did not come to dispossess the Arabs of the land, but to work together with them in peace and prosperity, for the good of all.

It is worth remembering, in Israel and beyond, that at the solemn proclamation of statehood, under savage onslaught still, we called upon the Arabs dwelling in Israel: "To keep the peace and to play their part in building the state on the basis of full and equal citizenship and due representation in all its institutions, provisional and permanent."

We extended "the hand of peace and good neighborliness to all the states around us and to their peoples," and we appealed to them "to cooperate in mutual helpfulness with the independent Jewish nation in its land and in a concerted effort for the advancement of the entire Middle East."

On 23 July, 1952, when King Farouk was deposed and the young officers, led by General Naguib, seized power in Egypt, hope sprang up in Israel that a new leaf had been turned in the neighborly relations between Egypt and ourselves, that we were entering an age of peace and cooperation. Prime Minister David Ben-Gurion, addressing the Knesset on 18 August, 1952, said:

> The state of Israel would like to see a free, independent and progressive Egypt, and we bear Egypt no grudge for what it did to our forefathers in Pharaoh's days, or even for what it did to us four years ago. Our goodwill toward Egypt—despite the Farouk government's foolish behavior toward us—has been demonstrated throughout the months of Egypt's involvement in a difficult conflict with a world power. And it never occurred

to us to exploit those difficulties and to attack Egypt or take revenge, as Egypt did to us upon the establishment of the state. And insofar as Egypt's present rulers are trying to uproot internal corruption and move their country forward to cultural and social progress, we extend to them our sincerest wishes for the success of their venture.

The answer came soon. Asked about Ben-Gurion's call for peace, Egypt's Prime Minister evaded the question, claiming that he knew no more than what he had read in the newspapers. Azzam, Secretary-General of the Arab League, said: "Ben-Gurion gave free flight to his imagination, which saw the invisible" (*Al-Misri*, 20 August, 1952). On 23 August, 1952, *Al-Ahram* explained that Israel had been forced to seek peace by a tottering economy, and proceeded: "In the past, on a number of occasions, Israel tried, at sessions of the Conciliation Commission, to sit with the Arabs around the table so as to settle existing problems. The Arabs refused, because they did not recognize the existence of the Jews, which is based on extortion."

We have never wearied of offering our neighbors an end to the bloody conflict and the opening of a chapter of peace and cooperation. All our calls have gone unheeded. Our proposals have been rejected in mockery and hatred. The policy of warring against us has persisted, with brief pauses, and thrice in a single generation forced hostilities upon us.

On 1 March, 1957, in the name of the government of Israel, I announced in the United Nations the withdrawal of our forces from territories occupied in the Sinai Campaign. I concluded with these words:

Can we, from now on—all of us—turn over a new leaf, and, instead of fighting with each other, can we all, united, fight poverty and disease and illiteracy? Is it possible for us to put all our efforts and all our energy into one single purpose, the ·betterment and progress and development of all our lands and all our peoples? I can here pledge the government and the people of Israel to do their part in this united effort. There is no limit to what we are prepared to contribute so that all of us, together, can live to see a day of happiness for our peoples and see again a great contribution from our region to peace and happiness for all humanity.

Ten years went by, of fedayeen activity, and once again we were confronted with the hazard of a surprise attack by Egypt, which had assembled powerful columns in eastern Sinai. The Six-Day War was fought, but when its battles ended, we did not behave as men drunk with victory, we did not call for vengeance, we did not demand the humiliation of the conquered. We knew that our real celebration would be on the day that peace comes. Instantly we turned to our neighbors, saying: "Our region is now at a crossroads: Let us sit down together, not as victors and conquered, but as equals; let us negotiate; let us determine secure and agreed boundaries; let us write a new page of peace, good neighborliness, and cooperation for the profit of all the nations of the Middle East."

The call was sounded over and over again in government statements, in declarations by the Prime Minister, the Deputy Prime Minister, the Foreign Minister, the Minister of Defense and other ministers—in the Knesset and in the United Nations, through all communication media. It was borne by emissaries, statesmen, authors, journalists, educators and by every means—public or covert—which seemed likely to bring it to our neighbors' ears.

The Knesset will not expect me to review the manifold efforts and attempts to establish any kind of contact with statesmen and competent authorities in the Arab countries. The people with whom we have tried, and shall again try, to open a dialogue do not want publicity. In this sensitive field, a hint of publication can be enough to extinguish a spark of hope. Imagination and a broad outlook are required, but imagination must not be allowed to become blindness. Patience and close attention are needed if seeds that have yet to germinate are to yield fruit in the course of time and not be sterilized by the glare of publicity. Our program includes the following points:

—The holy places of Christianity and Islam in Jerusalem to be placed under the responsibility of the respective faiths, with the aim of formulating agreements which will give force to their universal character;

—Mutual recognition of sovereignty;

—Regional cooperation in development projects for the good of the whole region.

The Arab leaders disregarded the program and did not even favor it with reply or comment.

On 17 March, 1969—the day on which I assumed my present office—I reemphasized the principles of peace, saying: "We are prepared to discuss peace with our neighbors, any day and on all matters."

Nasser's reply, three days later, was: "There is no voice transcending the sounds of war, and there must not be such a voice—nor is there any call holier than the call to war."

In the Knesset—on 5 May, 1969, on 8 May, and on 30 June—I reenunciated our readiness "to enter immediately into negotiations, without prior conditions, with every one of our neighbors, to reach a peace settlement."

The retort of the Arab states was swift. The commentators of Damascus, Amman, and Cairo stigmatized peace as "surrender" and heaped scorn on Israel's proposals. Take, for example, this from *Al-Destour,* a leading Jordanian newspaper, of 15 June, 1969: "Mrs. Meir is prepared to go to Cairo to hold discussions with President Abdul Nasser but, to her sorrow, has not been invited. She believes that one fine day a world without guns will emerge in the Middle East. Golda Meir is behaving like a grandmother telling bedtime stories to her grandchildren."

And that was the moment for Nasser to announce abrogation of the cease-fire agreements and nonrecognition of the cease-fire lines.

On 19 September, 1969, the Foreign Minister of Israel appealed in the United Nations to the Arab states "to declare their intention to establish a lasting peace, to eliminate the twenty-one-year-old conflict, to hold negotiations for detailed agreement on all the problems with which we are faced."

He referred to Israel's affirmation to Ambassador Jarring on 2 April: "Israel accepts the Security Council Resolution (242) calling for the promotion of agreement for the establishment of a just and lasting peace, reached through negotiation and agreement between the governments concerned. Implementation of the agreement will commence when accord has been reached on all its provisions."

On 24 September, 1969, during my visit to the United States, I was happy to hear that a statement had been made on behalf of the Egyptian Foreign Minister, then in New York, that Egypt was prepared to enter into Rhodes-style peace talks* with Israel. I responded forthwith that Israel was willing and, as previously recorded, was prepared to discuss the establishment of a true peace with Egypt at any time and without prior conditions.

Within a few hours, an authoritative démenti came from Cairo. Any Egyptian readiness to enter into Rhodes-style talks was officially denied. The spokesman of the Egyptian government termed the statement to that effect an "imperialist lie."

On 18 December, 1969, the Knesset approved the present government's basic principles. I quote the following passages:

> The government will steadfastly strive to achieve a durable peace with Israel's neighbors, founded on peace treaties achieved by direct negotiations between the parties. Agreed, secure, and recognized borders will be laid down in the treaties. The treaties will assure cooperation and mutual aid, the solution of any problem that may be a stumbling block on the path to peace, and the avoidance of all aggression direct and indirect. Israel will continue to be willing to negotiate—without prior conditions from either side—with any of the neighboring states for the conclusion of such a treaty. . . . The government will be alert for any expression of willingness amongst

---

* A reference to the armistice agreements signed by Egypt and Israel at Rhodes in 1949 under the United Nations chairmanship.

the Arab nations for peace with Israel and will welcome and respond to any readiness for peace from the Arab states. Israel will persevere in manifesting its peaceful intentions and in explaining the clear advantages to all the peoples of the area of peaceful coexistence, without aggression or subversion, without territorial expansion or intervention in the freedom and internal regimes of the states in the area.

In my address to the Knesset on 26 December, 1969, in the Foreign Minister's address to the Knesset on 7 April, 1970, and in a series of local press interviews on the eve of Passover and on the eve of Independence Day, that resolve was reaffirmed: "Day or night, if any sign whatever were to be seen, we would have responded to it."

Ambassador Jarring came and asked what Israel's response would be if he were to invite the foreign ministers to Cyprus or Geneva—and there was no hesitation on our part. He asked about Rhodes, and we said—let it be Rhodes.

In an interview published in *Ma'ariv* on 20 April I said: "We have no direct contacts with Egypt, but there are friends who travel around the world, to this place or that, statesmen who hate neither Israel nor Egypt. They tried to find a bridge, but could not."

On the contrary, there have been echoes of Nasser's speech of 1 May, 1970, making even the resumption of the cease-fire conditional on our total withdrawal and the return of the Palestinians to Israel.

These are but a few of our recurring solicitations for peace. We have not retracted one of them. We have not wearied of reiterating, day in, day out, our preparedness for peace. We have not abandoned hopes of finding a way into the hearts of our neighbors, though they yet dismiss our appeals with open animosity.

Today again, as the guns thunder, I address myself to our neighbors: Stop the killing; end the fire and bloodshed which bring tribulation and torment to all the peoples of the region!

End rejection of the cease-fire; end bombardment and raids; end terror and sabotage!

Even Russian pilots will not contrive to destroy the cease-fire lines, and certainly they will not bring peace. The only way to permanent peace and the establishment of secure and recognized boundaries is through negotiations between the Arab states and ourselves, as all sovereign states treat one another, as is the manner of states which recognize each other's right to existence and equality, as is the manner of free peoples, not protectorates enslaved to foreign powers or in thrall to the dark instincts of war, destruction, and ruin.

To attain peace, I am ready to go at any hour to any place, to meet any authorized leader of any Arab state—to conduct negotiations with mutual respect, in parity and without preconditions, and with a clear recognition that the problems under controversy can be solved. For there is room to fulfill the national aspirations of all the Arab states, and of Israel as well, in the Middle East, and progress, development, and cooperation can be hastened among all its nations, in place of barren bloodshed and war without end.

If peace does not yet reign, it is from no lack of willingness on our part; it is the inevitable outcome of the refusal of the Arab leadership to make peace with us. That refusal is still a projection of reluctance to be reconciled to the living presence of Israel within secure and recognized boundaries, still a product of the hope, which flickers on in their hearts, that they will accomplish its destruction. And this has been the state of things since 1948, long before the issue of the territories arose in the aftermath of the Six-Day War.

Moreover, if peace does not yet reign, it is equally not because of any lack of "flexibility" on our part, or because of the so-called "rigidity" of our position.

That position is: cease-fire, agreement, and peace. The Arab governments preach and practice no cease-fire, no negotiation, no agreement, and no peace. Which of the two attitudes is stubborn and unyielding: the Arab governments' or ours?

There are some, the Arabs included, who claim that we have not accepted the United Nations Resolution of 22 November, 1967, and that the Arabs have. In truth, the Arabs only accepted it in a distorted and mutilated interpretation of their own, as meaning an instant and absolute withdrawal of our forces, with no commitment to peace. They were ready to agree to an absolute Israeli withdrawal, but the resolution stipulates nothing of the kind. According to its text and the exegesis of its compilers, the resolution is not self-implementing. The operative clause calls for the appointment of an envoy, acting on behalf of the Secretary-General, whose task would be to "establish and maintain contact with the states concerned in order to promote agreement and assist efforts to achieve a peaceful and accepted settlement in accordance with the provisions and principles in this resolution." On 1 May, 1968, Israel's ambassador at the United Nations announced as follows:

> In declarations and statements made publicly and to Ambassador Jarring, the government of Israel has indicated its acceptance of the Security Council's resolution for the promotion of an agreement to establish a just and durable peace. I am authorized to reaffirm that we are willing to seek an agreement with each Arab state, on all the matters included in that resolution. More recently, we accepted Ambassador Jarring's proposal to arrange meetings between Israel and each of its neighbors, under his auspices, and in fulfillment of his mandate under the guidelines of the resolution to advance a peace agreement. No Arab state has yet accepted that proposal.

This announcement of our ambassador was reported to the House by the Foreign Minister on 29 May, 1968, and to the General Assembly in September, 1969. It opened the way for Ambassador Jarring to invite the parties to discuss any topic which any of them saw fit to raise, including issues mentioned in the resolution. The Arabs and those others who assert that we are preventing progress toward peace in terms of the resolution have no factual basis for so asserting. They seek merely to throw dust in the world's eyes, to cover up their guilt and deceive the world into thinking that we are the ones who are retarding peace.

It is also argued that, by creating facts on the ground, we are laying down irrevocable conditions which render negotiations superfluous or make it more difficult to enter into them. This contention, too, is wholly mistaken and unfounded. The refusal of the Arab states to enter into negotiations with us is simply an extension of their long-drawn-out intransigence. It goes back to before the Six-Day War, before there were any settlements in the administered territories.

After that fighting, we said—and we left no room for doubt—that we were willing to enter into negotiations with our neighbors with no preconditions on either side. This willingness does not signify that we have no opinions, thoughts, or demands or that we shall not exercise our right to articulate them in the discussions, as our neighbors are entitled to no less.

Nasser and Hussein, for example, in their official replies to Dr. Jarring, said that they saw the partition borders of 1947 as constituting definitive frontiers. I do not have to explain our attitude to that answer, but we do not insist that, in negotiating with us, the Arab states forfeit their equal right to make any proposal that they think fit, just as they cannot annul from the outset our right to express, in the discussions, any ideas or proposals which we may form. And there assuredly is no moral or political ground for demanding that we refrain from any constructive act in the territories, even though the Arab governments reject the call for peace and make ready for war.

There is yet another argument touching on our insistence on direct negotiations; it is as devoid as are the others of any least foundation in the annals of international relations or of those between our neighbors and ourselves. For we did sit down face to face with the representatives of the Arab states at the time of the negotiations in Rhodes, and no one dare profess that Arab honor was thereby affronted.

There is no precedent of a conflict between nations being brought to finality without direct negotiations. In the conflict between the Arabs and Israel, the issue of direct negotiations goes to the very crux of the matter. For the objective is to achieve peace and coexistence, and how will our neighbors ever be able to live with us in peace if they refuse to speak with us at all?

From the start of the conversations with Ambassador Jarring, we agreed that the face-to-face discussions should take place under the auspices of the Secretary-General's envoy. During 1968, Dr. Jarring sought to bring the parties together under his chairmanship in a neutral place. In March, 1968, he proposed that we meet Egypt and Jordan in Nicosia. We agreed, but the Arabs did not. In the same year, and again in September, 1969, we expressed our consent to his proposal that the meetings be held in the manner of the Rhodes talks, which comprised both face-to-face and indirect talks; a number of times it seemed that the Arabs and the Soviets would also fall in with that proposal, but in the end, they went back on it.

Only those who deny the right of another state to exist or who want to avoid recognizing the fact of its sovereignty can develop the refusal to talk to it into an inculcated philosophy of life which the pupil swears to adhere to as to a political, national principle. The refusal to talk to us directly is damning evidence that the unwillingness of the Arab leaders to be reconciled with the very being of Israel is the basic reason why peace is still to seek.

I am convinced that it is unreal and utopian to think that using the word "withdrawal" will pave the way to peace. True, those among us who do believe that the magic of that word is likely to bring us nearer to peace only mean withdrawal after peace is achieved and then only to secure and agreed boundaries demarcated in a peace treaty. On the other hand, when Arab and Soviet leaders talk of "withdrawal," they call for withdrawal without the making of a genuine peace and without any agreement on new permanent borders, but with an addendum calling for Israel's consent to the return of all the refugees.

Israel's policy is clear, and we shall continue to clarify it at every suitable opportunity, as we have done in the United

Nations and elsewhere. No person dedicated to truth could mis-
interpret our policy: When we speak of secure and recognized
boundaries, we do not mean that, after peace is made, the
Israel Defense Forces should be deployed beyond the boundaries agreed upon in negotiations with our neighbors. No one
could be misled—Israel desires secure and recognized boundaries with its neighbors.

Israel's Defense Forces have never crossed its borders in
search of conquest, but only when the safeguarding of the
existence and bounds of our state demanded it. Nasser's claim
that Israel wishes to maintain the cease-fire only so as to freeze
the cease-fire lines is preposterous. The cease-fire is necessary
not to perpetuate the lines, but to prevent death and destruction, to make progress easier toward a peace resting upon
secure and recognized boundaries. It is necessary as a step
upward on the ladder to peace. Incessant gunfire is a step down-
ward on the ladder to war.

The question is crystal clear, and there is no point in cloud-
ing it with semantics—or in trying to escape from reality. There
is not a single article in Israel's policy which prevents the
making of peace. Nothing is lacking for the making of peace
but the Arab persistence in denying Israel's very right to exist.
Arab refusal to acquiesce in our existence in the Middle East,
alongside the Arab states, abides. The only way to peace is
through a change in that recalcitrance.

When it changes, there will no longer be any obstacle to
peace negotiations. Otherwise, no formulae, sophistry, or def-
initions will avail. Those in the world who seek peace would
do well to heed this basic fact and help to bring about a change
in the obdurate Arab approach, which is the real impediment
to peace. Any display of "understanding" and forgiveness, however unwitting, is bound to harden the Arabs in their obstinacy
and hearten them in their gainsaying of Israel's right to exist
and will, besides, be exploited by Arab leaders to justify
ideologically the continuance of the war against Israel.

Nothing unites our people more than the desire for peace.
There is no stronger urge in Israel, and on joyful occasions and

in hours of mourning alike it is expressed. Nothing can wrench out of our hearts or out of our policy this wish for peace, this hope of peace—not even our indignation over the killing of our loved ones, not even the enmity of the rulers of the Arab world.

The victories that we have won have never intoxicated us or filled us with such complacency as to relinquish the wish and call for peace—a peace that means good neighborly relations, cooperation and an end to slaughter. Peace and coexistence with the Arab peoples have been, and are, among the fundamentals of Jewish renaissance. Generations of the Zionist movement were brought up on them. The desire for peace has charted the policy of all Israel's governments, of whatever membership. No government of Israel in power, however constituted, has ever blocked the way to peace.

With all my heart, I am convinced that in Israel, in the future as in the past, there could be no government which would not bespeak the people's cardinal and steadfast aspirations to bring about a true and enduring peace.

22. Labor in a Time of Crisis

A statement made on December 12, 1969, at the Eleventh Histadrut Congress in Tel Aviv. (In Hebrew)

No issue unique to a trade union was ever the chief or only theme for discussion at the Histadrut's conferences and councils. This failure was not due to a disregard of the workers' vital bread-and-butter interests. Ever since the Histadrut first came into being, even before its formal establishment, when the workers of Palestine were still few and isolated, they undertook to be the vanguard of the nation. No one imposed this task on them; no official forum elected the pioneer workers of Palestine for this mission.

Having come with the Second Aliyah, they were not the first Jewish settlers. But theirs was the primary path; they and those who followed in the Third Aliyah and subsequent waves of immigration set themselves one undeviating rule: to implement first the goals important for the nation's existence and the up-building of the homeland. The strength of the workers was expressed in this emphasis. Adherence to this priority—not empty platitudes, not big words and small deeds, but an absolute commitment to all that was fundamental for the building of a nation—formed the basis for the path followed by the workers of Israel. Only later did the countless achievements of the trade union movement come into being.

It was at Histadrut meetings that all the resolutions which

preserved the nation, every struggle, every act of volunteering —without which we would never have reached our present stride—were debated and determined. It is not surprising therefore that the Jews of the Diaspora, including many who did not accept the ideology of the workers' movement, gave their faith and help to the Labor Federation throughout the years. This confidence was reflected officially in the Zionist congresses and sprang from an awareness that for the sake of Zionism, in practice, as well as in theory, it was necessary to lend support to the chief implementers of the national idea.

It was the Histadrut which dispatched its members as volunteers to every settlement in need of protection or other help. It was the Histadrut which perceived the importance of the small deeds that added together formed one great act of creation. Even during our struggle for independence we knew enough to appreciate every positive act, small as well as big. Now there is no Jew, in Israel or abroad, who does not realize that those tiny, isolated settlements in tents and huts scattered throughout the expanses of the Negev halted the invading Egyptian Army.

It was the Histadrut which sought to help European Jewry immediately upon our learning of the Holocaust. I should like to recall a comrade, long departed, Comrade Neistadt (Noy), who was first sent by the Histadrut's Central Committee to Ankara, to seek any means possible to reach Jews in the ghettos and concentration camps in the occupied countries. It was from the offices of the Executive Committee of the Histadrut that the volunteer parachutists—Hannah Senesh, Aviva Reik, Enzo Sereni, and others—set out in order to rescue the few survivors. I recall the gathering at the offices of the Executive Committee of the Histadrut, of those members who volunteered to fight the Nazis; they received our blessing together with a modest gift, a Bible. Many did not return.

The Histadrut continued along this path in the knowledge that it was a large body which could not absolve itself of the responsibility it had undertaken both toward what had already been achieved in Israel and particularly toward that which had not yet been accomplished. Now that the Histadrut has become the Labor Federation of Israel, in an independent state, I ask that we avoid a serious danger. We must not nurture the illusion that because the state exists, with a Knesset and a government, we no longer need regard ourselves as a body concerned with every aspect of life in Israel (and let no one suspect me of being unaware of the function and place of the Knesset, the government, and the various administrative authorities). I pray, therefore, that no member sitting here as a representative of a large community of a million and more workers (whose number is increasing daily) will cherish the illusion that he is no longer responsible for all that exists and for what should come into being. We can have no strong state able to stand fast without the total commitment of organized labor. Since we are still far from peace and quiet and are faced by difficult and grave struggles, every one of us in the Histadrut must undertake fullest responsibility as in the past.

We are still at war. We have gained a great military victory, a victory of deliverance. It is important that we recall the threat of total extermination, particularly today, when we are told that it is not "nice" to gain territories secured by war: as if this nation arose one fine day and decided that it had to conquer; as if we had not been threatened by actual physical danger; as if millions throughout the world did not wait in trepidation, fearing what might happen to the people of Israel.

I do not believe that all this is forgotten. We did not engage in a war for the conquest of territory: we faced total annihilation. And yet we are now being preached to; we are informed that "expansion" is improper and that the issue is being weighed in the scales of "justice." Our neighbors, however, do not want peace and are preparing for war, and because of the contradiction existing between us and them—our desire for peace against the lack of a similar desire on their part—there is no peace in our region. Surely it is not necessary to recall that to this very day not a single Arab ruler has been found who has uttered one simple sentence: "I am prepared for true peace with the state of Israel." To our regret, no such sentence has been uttered, and no good can come from the attempt of other powers to pronounce these words on behalf of the Arab states. The rulers who led their nations to war against us to annihilate us—they and only they must express a wish to lead their nations to peace with us.

We voiced our longing for peace immediately after the war and have never ceased voicing it since then; we reiterate it day by day. Even those who vilify us, referring to us as "Zionist imperialists," know in their hearts that Israel wants peace. But since we are a people tried by catastrophe and war, we are no longer ready to accept the illusion of peace instead of true peace.

We still have many great tasks facing us. For the sake of the millions of Jews who are not here—the Jews in the Soviet Union, those still remaining in the Arab countries, and those dispersed in the free countries—for their sake, too, we must recall, that the majority of the Jewish people is not yet in its homeland; and who better than we know that only here in Israel can a full, proud, and secure Jewish life be led? No force in the world can destroy the aspiration of Jews—wherever they may be—to freedom, to independence, to an upright posture. They can be persecuted, they can be expelled to Siberia, they can be arrested and threatened, they can be the victims of incitement and hate—but their spirit cannot be suppressed. Under whatever regime Jews live, they display the strength steadfastly to withstand their oppressors and enemies.

Here in Israel we are still in a state of war. The Israel Defense Forces still man the borders, near settlements ignorant of what the next hour holds in store. Will it be possible to work in the fields? Words cannot be found to express our pride, concern, and love for the members of these settlements and for those at the front. At my age it may be permissible for me to refer to these soldiers, the eighteen- and nineteen-year-old boys and girls, as children, and to say that they—these children—become heroes overnight. I correspond with a girl in the third grade at Yardena. Children of this age are not content with written words, so she sends me letters including drawings of flowers and other ornaments, covering the envelopes as well. This child, whom I do not know personally, sends me an account: "There was a shelling. We ran to the shelter, and again there was a shelling and cottage was hit." In conclusion, she remarks: "Do not worry, morale is high."

Anyone pretending to know when this situation will end is uttering a falsehood. Not one of us knows, and if truth be told —how I wish we were proven wrong!—the situation is likely to last a long time; much strength will be needed to endure. But we must not yield to illusions, such as one nurtured among us by those who preach acceptance of the Security Council resolution whose Arab interpretation according to Nasser is that Israel must withdraw to the 1967 border. Nor does Nasser even add that if Israel does so he will conduct peace negotiations with Israel. *This he does not say.* When friends preach to us that we are not comporting ourselves properly, that possibly all required to make the 1967 border a secure frontier is an adjustment here or there, we must ask them: Why would the 1967 border suddenly become secure? After all, that was the frontier along which we stood until 5 June, 1967, and it was from beyond that very frontier that the Arabs set out to destroy us. Would this same border be more secure now than on that day? For the sake of our very existence, it is imperative that our border be secure. It is not true to charge that expansion is our aim: as if that is why there is a dispute between us and our neighbors; as if three wars broke out because of territory. Here are the facts: In 1947 we agreed to a frontier; it was destroyed by the Arab countries; again in 1967 there was a frontier; this, too, was destroyed by the Arabs; and now, even if we are forced to insist thereon for years, we will under no circumstances agree to a settlement which provides for less than true peace. We will not agree to borders which would again facilitate renewed Arab attacks, and we will not with our own hands pave the way for a fourth war. All that we want is exactly what nations throughout the world possess: peace with defensible borders. I know it is no simple matter to state that we must continue to hold onto the existing frontiers, since this is far from easy along the border and in the new settlements. However, such a declaration must be accompanied by an awareness of the significance of our stand, which requires heroism and preparedness for trial not only on the part of our children, but on the part of the parents as well.

We have no "uncle" to give us what we need on a "silver platter." By very great efforts, involving tremendous tension, we are trying to secure from one source or another (and there are not many to choose from), those essentials without which it is impossible to protect the state and safeguard its existence and our lives. At this juncture the Histadrut must effect a change in a situation no longer bearable in this country—the gap between front line and rear, a gap whose existence among us is inestimably graver than it would be for other nations. It is inconceivable that a home from which a boy sets out for the Suez Canal or the Jordan Valley, for the Golan Heights or any other spot such as the *Nahal* outposts which are also on the firing line—it is inconceivable that such a home, with all its display of concern at every telephone call, every doorbell, should not truly participate in every phase of the national need. After all—without platitude—our Army is a true army of the people, and these boys are the sons of us all.

There are friends who ask us: "How will you be able to withstand the pressure?" And we try to explain: We shall withstand because we have no alternative. To Jews I reply: "As long as you stand fast, so shall we; you also have no alternative but to stand together with us." But to you I say: There is no moral validity in demanding this fortitude only of the working community. The entire nation is mobilized, and the front line is everywhere. The strength of a society—if it is decent and just —finds expression in tolerating no gap in its total stand.

Believe me, I am far removed from pessimism. I ask only that we should not escape facts. We have never fled from the front line or abandoned any place. It is wonderful that not one person has fled from Beisan, Kiryat Shmonah, or other moshavim and kibbutzim located along the border. I am nearly fifty years in Israel and I have never despaired. I have never given in to pessimism, and certainly not now. But I know what faces us, and there is no secret knowledge involved. Every one of you, just like me, knows what faces us and what can keep us. The best of friends, even if they wished, could not do so in our stead. We do not want others to fight our war, but we have the right to demand of nations whose policy is not anti-Semitic that they help us, so that we should not confront better tanks and more numerous and superior guns and planes emptyhanded. Though this world is not as lovely and righteous as it might be, here and there it still holds a friendly nation to whom we may turn with our just demands.

In comparing our present situation with others in the past, I bear in mind that we have never truly enjoyed peace. The difference is that in the past we were very few and poor in the face of the animosity and hatred directed against us, whereas today—for all the vast danger—we are greater in number. A million of us are already organized in a unified community of workers. There are, admittedly, differences of opinion within this organization; however, even the size and nature of the dissent prove the extent to which this Histadrut of a million members is consolidated and prepared to face its challenges as was the case in the past.

I hope that we will meet in future and recall this conference, noting the fact that the continued existence of the Jewish people depended on us as in the past. This awareness of responsibility for the national welfare will increase our strength to face all situations in the future. I pray that the example provided by the founders of our labor movement will always guide us so that this Histadrut will not forfeit by as much as a hairsbreadth the sense of national and social mission which is its charge as a body and that of its members individually.

23. Poverty in Israel

A discussion of Israel's pressing social problems given in the Knesset. (In Hebrew, July 28, 1971)

Much has been written recently on what is referred to in Israel as "the communal problem." In addition to considered statements, there have been some containing a considerable degree of exaggeration and unfairness; some of these have been calculated, not to help in the solution of the problems and the achievement of national unity but, on the contrary, to fan the flames of intercommunal tension. From this standpoint there is no difference whether such unfortunate statements are made by an Ashkenazi about the Sephardi* community or a Sephardi about the Ashkenazim.

I shall not quote these statements, thus obviating the need to reply to them one by one, but I regard it as a supreme duty to urge all of us to express ourselves in a responsible and considered manner when discussing this painful subject in our lives. I should be the last person in the world to hide from reality and declare that the problem does not exist and that Israel has already achieved the longed-for equality among the various communities that have been gathered here from the dispersions of the exile.

* Ashkenazim are Jews of German-European or Western origin. Sephardim are Jews of Spanish or Portuguese origin; sometimes the term is used to designate Oriental Jews.

We realize the disparity in status when we inquire what is the percentage of students from the Sephardi communities in the universities and institutions of higher learning, when we study the housing situation of large families and other areas, but just as it is wrong to ignore the problem, so can there be no greater distortion of the truth than to say that the existing situation is the result of an Israeli policy or of calculated discrimination.

Many immigrants from the Islamic countries brought the results of deprivation and discrimination with them in their "baggage" from their countries of origin. The Jews who came to us from the Islamic countries were of a higher cultural level than the populations from which they came, but it was their fate to live in countries that had not yet developed industrially and culturally, and they were deprived of the opportunity to develop their special characteristics, to express their intellectual capacity, and to acquire the education that was given to those coming from the developed countries of Europe and America.

Only when we see the achievements of many members of the Oriental communities under Israeli conditions can we realize what talents were suppressed among Jews in the Islamic countries because of the low level of development there. Is it their fault that fate was unkind to them as a result of the vicissitudes of Jewish history? The immigration to Israel of our brothers from the Islamic countries put an end to the backwardness and repression which was their fate for centuries. A new phase opened in their annals and in the development of our people as a whole.

Due to the conditions in their country of residence, Jewish women from Yemen arrived here in almost every case unable to read and write. I refer particularly to the women, for their husbands who came from Yemen all knew how to pray and were versed in religious learning, and their children were taught in religious schools. I remember a child aged eleven or twelve whom I met in a transit camp in Galilee shortly after he came to Israel. The child spoke Hebrew; when I asked him where he had learned the language, he replied proudly: "I know the Bible—Hebrew from the Bible." It was, therefore, a basic human and cultural revolution when women from the Islamic countries went to school in Israel and began to learn to read and write, and when young women in the armed forces became devoted teachers of our sisters from Yemen.

Of the authentic Jewish character of the Jews of Yemen, of North Africa or Iraq, there is no need to speak at length. Their willingness to give their lives for the nation and its homeland is a shining chapter in our history. Not long ago I had the opportunity of meeting a young man who came from Iraq only a year ago and who told me of bestial tortures which he and his friends had undergone in jail in Baghdad because of "Zionism." I was amazed at how they withstood the tortures and the interrogations, not uttering a word for fear of harming the state of Israel. I recall similar reports by comrades who had returned from missions to Iraq, comrades who laid the foundations there for the organization of Jewish Youth for Self-Defense and Pioneering.

Among the emissaries to the Islamic countries there were also Ashkenazim, Jews from the West. All of the emissaries operated at personal risk. Did they take this grave risk to bring their brothers to Israel because they wanted them to suffer discrimination?

It must unfortunately be admitted that the great enterprise of immigrant absorption, an enterprise unparalleled anywhere in the world in scope, expenditure, and effort, has not been sufficient to bridge the inequalities the immigrants brought with them from the various parts of the world. The time span, too, has been inadequate. To our gratification, enormous progress has been made, but it is not enough. We must not be content with what has been achieved. However, anyone who fails to see what has been achieved—anyone who ignores the progress made is either ignorant or knowingly denies the facts.

In the course of my duties as Minister of Labor in the years 1949–56, I saw conditions at first hand. We have come a long way from the immigrant camps set up at Shaar Ha'aliyah near Haifa, at Bet Lid and Pardess Hanna, and the transit camps near Petah Tikvah and in Jerusalem, to the situation prevailing now. In March, 1949, over 200,000 people were living in tents in the camps, often two families to a tent. In 1949 there were no sources of employment. We did not inherit housing from the mandatory government. There was no food in the stores, and above all, when mass immigration began, we were at the climax of the War of Independence.

It was an unparalleled act of boldness when the late Levi Eshkol initiated the dissolution of the first camps and the transfer of the immigrants to transitional quarters, from tents to canvas, corrugated iron, and wooden huts. We had to import the materials for this modest building program, and while distress was great, so was the momentum. The overwhelming majority of the newcomers had no experience in any vocation— I am not referring to the professions, but to building, farming, and factory work. And let there be no misunderstanding: In those tents and later in the transitional quarters were Western and Oriental Jews, both the remnants of the Holocaust who had come from the refugee camps in Europe and the detention camps in Cyprus and Jews from the ghettos in the Islamic countries.

I well remember the early buildings, the "palaces" of those times: cinder-block houses of 28 and 32 square meters. Yet compared with the black tents and the notorious canvas huts, these were truly palaces. A trained labor force to build the cinder-block houses did not yet exist among the new immigrants. We should give due credit to the veteran construction workers who came forward to train the immigrants and to build. At the same time we undertook the enormous settlement enterprise of establishing hundreds of villages in the north and south. For the majority of the immigrants this was their first contact with work on the soil. They had to produce bread from the ground not by prayer but by labor. I am still amazed at how quickly these new farmers became not only a decisive factor in the supply of food to our people but also an important factor in agricultural export; their produce finds its way to the markets of Europe.

I remember the first teachers who undertook to teach the children just recently arrived in the country and the huts in Kiryat Shmonah which served as the first schools. I recall the beginnings of Migdal Ha'Emek, Dimona, Kiryat Gat, and the Beersheba of those days, with its primitive tents and huts. Now, when I see the nurses in Beersheba Hospital, the factory workers, the students, and schoolchildren, it is hard to believe that these are the same urchins who ran through those sands. Does anyone honestly believe that a revolution of this kind with its diverse cultural, economic, and social manifestations can reach completion in twenty years? Is there an example of such a monumental change in other countries?

I would not for a moment claim that the job is done. There is much to do, much to add in Kiryat Shmonah, Migdal Ha'Emek, Kiryat Malachi, and Beersheba, in the development towns and the suburbs of the large cities. But is it fair to ignore what has been achieved in these years? Denial and belittlement will not increase the rate of progress.

This great work was done not merely thanks to the aid of the veteran settlers. Without an effort by the immigrants themselves, without their efficient cooperation, it could not have been accomplished, just as it would not have been done without the constant aid of the government and other public bodies. Our endeavor to overcome the specific hardships of the various communities must continue, from both the economic and the social points of view. This attempt on the part of the government of Israel will not stop but will steadily increase in scope.

We cannot deny that poverty exists in Israel; we must not accept this situation. We would be false to ourselves if we became accustomed to its presence and regarded it with complacency. Zionism has always been imbued with an aspiration for social justice, for both a national and social renaissance.

Beyond doubt the two issues that call for a special effort are housing and education. Our education laws apply in equal measure to all children in Israel, yet it cannot be said that this equality is implemented in practice. We cannot claim that there is equality between two children studying in the same class and with the same teacher, if one comes from a home in which four persons live in three rooms, with a houseful of books and parents able to assist in the preparation and homework, while his classmate comes from a two-room house with ten inhabitants, with no one able to help the child to make progress in his studies. There is no genuine equality between these two children. We have known problems which we have succeeded in solving. And there are complex problems which, despite all efforts, will take a long time to solve. Material resources can speed up the pace, but sometimes even financial resources cannot do the work of time.

A massive housing program has been carried out in Israel. In the period 1949–1970, over 400,000 units of public housing were built. Today, there is no place in Israel—not even the most isolated—which has no school, kindergarten, and in most cases a nursery school as well. There are not many places in the world where free education is provided to children aged three or four.

Since the establishment of the state, we have been blessed with ministers of education endowed with vision, who have seen it as a mission of the first importance to overcome the educational and cultural gap among our citizens. Israel's ministers of education, beginning with President Shazar, each regarded this objective as his first duty. Not all the goals have been attained, but there has been steady progress.

Is it an insignificant achievement that thanks to a system of graduated fees the secondary schools include over 50 percent of children who are totally exempt from paying fees? Now we have a problem of dropouts to be tackled. But the percentage of dropouts has been declining in the last few years. It is a gross distortion of the truth to allege that the state's initiative in dealing with the problem of disadvantaged groups is a result of vocal demonstrations which have recently taken place. Could hundreds of thousands of housing units be built overnight? Could schools suddenly sprout all over the country? Could long-standing vocational training be the outcome of demonstrations, or the network of hospitals spread all over the country be the product of pressure by this or that group? In Israel today almost 100 percent of mothers give birth under first-class medical supervision. I can recall the days when women in the tents of Bet Lid refused to go to a hospital to give birth.

Progress in housing, education, and health services was achieved through the supreme effort of the people and the government of Israel, although the country never had one day free of anxiety for its security and survival. All was accomplished in the midst of actual warfare and in periods of terrorism between wars.

What of our "nondeprived"? When I follow developments among us in the social sphere, I sometimes ask myself: What has happened to us in the past year? We are a wise, sensible, and patriotic people, who can reach heights of self-sacrifice; without such qualities we would not have established the state, and we would not have survived. What has happened to our good sense? To our self-discipline? We are behaving as if there were no danger ahead of us, as if we had already achieved the peace we long for, as if we had already eliminated poverty and completed the development of the country, as if we did not have to prepare ourselves for the further immigration bound to arrive.

I stated earlier that there is poverty in Israel. That is a fact. And I add: There is wealth, and that is also a fact. We are faced with a supreme need to develop the economy, for only in the development of our economy is there hope for a better economic situation for us all. We also need investments from abroad, for we cannot develop the economy from our own resources alone to the extent necessary to absorb immigration— and the need for continued immigration remains paramount. In order to invite investments, we must make reasonable profits possible. Yet despite this need, and our progressive taxation system, there are people in Israel who live above the standard of living we may permit ourselves. They are not numerous, but they exist. Is it too much to ask the contractor, the industrialist, the wholesaler to look to their own conduct, so that not only laws will regulate what is permitted and what is forbidden, but they themselves will look after quality, price, the avoidance of exorbitant profits, correct weight, and good service.

I was brought up in the labor movement, and I have always looked upon the Histadrut as not merely a trade union but as a united body duty bound to lead in the struggle for social justice. Our sense of social justice, our alertness to the need for a proper standard of living in the Histadrut, the government, and the Knesset have not been blunted, nor will they be, and thereby we have served the entire nation.

I believe we all agree that there has been no decline in the standard of living in any sector in the country. The standard of living has risen for everyone in the period between the wars and during the wars. Greater and stronger nations did not raise their population's standard of living when faced by a war for survival. (We must bear in mind the fact that it is in no small measure thanks to world Jewry that we could afford this rise despite war and immigrant absorption.) A trade union is not only entitled, it is obliged, to safeguard the worker's rights and assure him of a just reward for his output. But one of the primary considerations in labor relations, an absolute condition for social stability and for a democratic regime, is the strict honoring of labor agreements. It is natural to conduct stubborn negotiations for the conclusion of an agreement. It is legitimate to insist on rights, including the adoption of the strike weapon if negotiations are protracted and no agreement is reached. But once an agreement is signed, it must be honored. This obligation applies to both employer and employees.

To my regret we have recently witnessed a phenomenon which must on no account be countenanced. After an agreement is signed, a new round of claims is immediately submitted. Such a situation is many times more serious when it affects the public sector and when the employer is not a profit earner, but the state itself. I am well aware that among wage earners and government employees there are no individuals or groups whose earnings furnish them a life of ease. I am not claiming that we are free of want and distress among workers. I know about low rates of wages. I live among the working people, and I am acquainted with their problems. But this situation does not absolve any side from the duty of honoring agreements.

The public knows that there is a war on, that a defense budget is needed, which imposes a burden the like of which does not exist in any country, and it is sensitive to social problems and the paramount need to act for the eradication of poverty. Therefore, I cannot understand how the most essential services can be paralyzed by strikes, three or four months after an agreement has been signed. The situation which has arisen recently is fraught with danger to Israeli society and the foundation of our existence. For my own part, I believe that the state has an obligation, even in time of war, to raise the standard of living of those strata which are really in need. Those sections that are on the verge of poverty, earning the lowest salaries, are entitled to our aid, with whatever can be provided from the national budget after defense needs and the basic requirements of survival have been met. Whatever may be allocated to salary increases should be directed exclusively to those strata. And all those among us whose standard of living is higher should remain, despite hardship, at the same level until things get better.

I have never supported, nor do I support, the sanctity of the salary gap and the differentials which have taken root in our lives. According to that view, if the low-wage earners get an increase, everyone must receive an increase, right up the ladder to the top, to avoid infringing on the principle of differentials. Unfortunately, the principle of differentials is insisted upon in all sectors, among the staffs of public services, banks, institutions, and companies, both private and public.

In time of war our people displays a supreme capacity for voluntary effort, self-restraint, and sacrifice. In view of the equality of all of us in the face of danger, what is the point of this insistence on the sanctity of differentials, which hampers the improvement of living standards among the underpaid? I am not preaching a return to the austere atmosphere of days gone by and past concepts of dress and entertainment. But I must warn against the gap between a life-style imported from abroad which is taking root in Israel, especially among the higher-income strata, and our real national economic capacity. This is a dangerous and ominous gap.

Many strikes are declared not by those on the lowest rung of the income ladder, but by the best-situated among the wage earners, members of the liberal professions, skilled workmen whose pay is not low, workers who occupy key positions and who, if they strike, may impede or paralyze the country's most vital services. The undermining of labor relations in Israel arouses grave anxiety in the hearts of all, even those who do not share governmental responsibility. Breakdowns in vital services spread depression among the public.

The government cannot remain inactive in this situation. Throughout the years I have believed, and I still believe, in the right of the organized worker to freedom of collective bargaining and in the rule of agreements and contracts in labor relations. I still believe today that only such a rule is practicable in a democratic society in which private enterprise exists.

For many years I opposed legislation on strikes, and I hoped that in our country labor relations would be regulated without recourse to such legislation. I must admit that after recent events, I have begun to doubt. Under the pressure of necessity, we were compelled to decide on restraining orders for the purpose of preventing loss of life due to stoppages in hospitals.

In labor relations I do not intend to place our trust in commands and laws, but I am convinced that the Knesset and the Israel government cannot neglect their obligations. With the help of the General Federation of Labor and together with the employers—whether private or public—we must find ways to regulate labor relations on a basis of social justice, the strict observance of labor agreements and within the scope of our economic capacity.

I fear that we may lose our sense of proportion between the desirable and the possible. We must call a halt and consider where we are going. Is it realistic to assume that without consideration for the country's position, without a readiness for self-restraint on the part of all of us—first and foremost, of those who stand on the highest rungs of the income and salary ladder—the government can, as with a magic wand, meet all demands: eradicate poverty, not impose taxes, win wars, absorb immigration, develop the economy? Can the government—any government—do all these things at one and the same time?

While discussing poverty, it has been argued lately that the absorption of new immigrants injures the veteran residents of Israel. I believe that there can be no greater and more dangerous distortion of the truth than this shameful argument. Zionism has taught us that no immigrant does Israel a favor by coming here and that the state does the immigrant no favor by absorbing him. This concept is the ideological and actual basis for the existence and mission of the state.

Always in the past, under all circumstances, veteran settlers received newcomers willingly, of their own free choice, as the natural outcome of their Zionist aspirations. Even when we built cinder-block huts for new immigrants, there were veteran families in Israel living in the most wretched housing conditions, two and three families to an apartment, with a joint kitchen and a communal bathroom. In '49 and '50 the veteran settler accepted strict rationing so that the little we had would be divided justly between newcomers and old settlers.

The veterans did the immigrants no favor. Our undertaking was never limited to meeting the needs of those who were already here. In the same way young immigrants of military age begin their service as soon as they arrive in the homeland. This is the basis for our unity and our people's partnership of destiny.

It is precisely those among us who are truly worried by the problem of poverty who must fight with all their moral strength against the disgraceful argument which presents the absorption of immigrants as an obstacle to the solution of Israel's social problems. We must let no one, either in bitterness or in malice, raise a false barrier between those who came yesterday and those who are arriving today and will arrive tomorrow.

Finally, in the campaign for the eradication of poverty, as in the effort to solve the problems of underprivileged youth, two partners are required. In the first place, the personal effort of those among us who themselves suffer from poverty is needed. They must not allow themselves to become passive objects. They must be active factors in the effort to change their situation and join with the general public and the government in this effort. Secondly, all sections of the settled population, adults and youth, must join in a great volunteer movement to seek out disadvantaged youth in their homes—in good fellowship, in a sincere desire to help—so as to achieve social integration and training. Otherwise, it is doubtful whether we can achieve a solution and arrive at greater equality in Israeli society.

Social equality cannot be attained merely with material resources. Those who have knowledge and education must be ready and willing to share with those who lack them, for inequality in money and property is not always the most tragic. There is an even more crying inequality—between those who know and those who do not know.

We are a nation of volunteers. Volunteering is the foundation for our entire renaissance movement. This spirit must be aroused among all strata of the nation: women's organizations and youth movements, individuals and organized groups. There must be a continued and intensified effort by the government, combined with the utmost voluntary effort. Only so can we achieve the society which we all desire: only so shall we be faithful to the character and mission of the state of Israel.

24. Let My People Go

A statement in the Knesset in regard to the Leningrad trials of Soviet Jews accused of seeking to emigrate to Israel. (In Hebrew, May 17, 1971)

The sole guilt of the Leningrad defendants is their wish to emigrate to Israel, their aspiration to be united with their people in its homeland. These Jews are not acting against the Soviet regime. They do not constitute an anti-Soviet underground. Their only crime is the study of Hebrew, love of Hebrew literature, and reading an "underground" book such as *Exodus*. They have no intention of concealing the love for Israel which is in their hearts. They do not wish to be different from or inferior to the members of other nationalities in the Soviet Union. They sign petitions openly, giving their addresses.

The attempt to present the desire to emigrate to Israel as if it were a plot against the Soviet regime is both ridiculous and criminal. This claim is not merely an anti-Zionist libel, but also an incitement against Jews all over the world—as if the desire to emigrate to Israel, which is the birthright of Jews everywhere, were restricted to the USSR alone. Any attempt to suppress the aspiration toward Zion can only lead to the adoption of criminal methods unworthy of an enlightened society, whatever its regime. This policy stands in direct contradiction to the basic rights of man. Men should not be tried for their aspirations, for the fact that they seek recognition of their human rights and are fighting by legal means to have these rights recognized.

On the eve of the Soviet Communist Party Congress, the Soviet authorities increased the number of permits for emigration to Israel. The number of immigrants who then arrived surpassed what we had previously been accustomed to, for which we gave thanks with all our hearts. This was not merely an act of justice toward the Jews wishing to emigrate to Israel —it was an act arousing sympathy. To our great regret, however, the Leningrad trial once again proves that we cannot remain calm. Instead of the authorities behaving in accordance with common sense and basic human rights and allowing the Leningrad defendants to emigrate to Israel, as some of their friends had been allowed to do, the trial proves that the terrible system of threat and terror, calculated to break the will of those who love and long for Zion, continues.

All of us are worried and disturbed; all of us are angry.

None of us has forgotten, nor can forget, what trials in the Soviet Union presage. How can we distract our minds from what happened at the first Leningrad trial? Enlightened public opinion the world over raised an angry outcry against the savage sentences. The defendants who had been condemned to death had their sentences commuted, but this cannot lighten our anxiety. They received long prison terms, and the whole world knows what suffering incarceration in a Soviet prison entails.

We repeat: The aim of these trials is not merely to try the accused, but over and above that to spread fear and terror among the others, so that they should not dare to express their longing to emigrate to Israel.

The more we meet our brothers, the more convinced are we that the national revival among Soviet Jewry is very deep-rooted and widespread. It is vain to expect that this marvelous awakening can be suppressed by arbitrary means. This awakening draws its strength from our people's age-long history. It is nurtured by the lessons of the Holocaust on the one hand, and by the miracle of Israel's rebirth on the other. Violent methods have the power to cause suffering, bitterness, and rage, but they cannot block the springs of the awakening.

Yesterday all the members of the Cabinet went to the Western Wall to shake the hands of the immigrants who are keeping vigil there as a sign of protest. By this warm handclasp we sought to express our total solidarity with the innocent defendants and with every Jew in the Soviet Union who may stand in the dock for the crime of longing for Zion and Israel.

We protest at a method of oppression which exploits law and jurisprudence in the service of a cynical and cruel policy. We feel that we have the right and duty to call upon the nations of the world not to keep silent, not to stand idly by. We call for an intensification of this just and responsible struggle by all public means worthy of this sacred goal. In spite of the callousness of the Soviet authorities, there is a chance that a worldwide struggle will not remain without influence, but will bear fruit. Let us not allow habit and fatigue to weaken this just struggle.

From this rostrum we call on governments, parliaments, clergymen, teachers and educators, students and youth, on right-minded public opinion throughout the world, to raise their voices and to approach the Soviet authorities with the demand that those authorities cease this unacceptable system of trials against Jews arraigned for the crime of desiring to emigrate to Israel and to free these innocent accused. The right of a Jew who so wishes to emigrate to his people's homeland, is a natural right which the Soviet Union must recognize. The struggle for the recognition of this right is legitimate and deserves the support of all who seek justice and believe in human rights.

To those on trial, we say: For months you have been imprisoned in absolute isolation, but I believe that despite your isolation, you feel that you are not cut off from us, just as we feel that we are united with you. We are all sitting alongside you in the dock for the crime of loyalty to Zion and Israel. The blessing and support of Israel, and of Jews everywhere, go out to you.

25. At the Western Wall

On receiving the Freedom of Jerusalem. (In Hebrew, 1971)

In a few weeks it will be fifty years since I came to this country. Naturally, a short time after my arrival in 1921, I went up to Jerusalem, and when one comes to Jerusalem one goes first to the Western Wall. Who raised in a Jewish home could have failed to absorb Jerusalem into his being, with all that the Western Wall symbolizes? I too grew up in a good traditional Jewish house, yet I was not myself pious, and I confess that I went to the Wall without much emotion.

Many of you remember the narrow, winding alleys of those days. I stood in front of the Wall—then much smaller than the present large excavated expanse—I saw Jews, men and women, praying and weeping, putting their *kvitlech,* their notes, into the crannies of the old stones. Then I suddenly understood its magic. This ruin was all that was left of a glory that once had been; it was tragic that only this remained. But in those Jews and Jewesses, with their *kvitlech,* I saw a refusal to accept the fact that only these stones were left; these *kvitlech* were an expression of confidence in a future to come. That is what made the ruin strong, and I left the Wall changed in feeling.

For nineteen years—from 1948 to 1967—we in Israel could not enter the Old City and East Jerusalem; we could not go to the Wall; we could only watch the desecration of the Mount of Olives from a distance. Then came the Six-Day War, and on a Wednesday we were all electrified with the news that the Old City had been liberated. I had to fly to the United States that Friday morning. I decided I could not leave without visiting the Old City and going to the Western Wall. So on that Friday, when civilians were not yet allowed to enter the Old City because there was still shooting, I received a permit to enter. That June I was not in the government but a civilian like any other. I went to the Wall together with some soldiers.

There, in that narrow alley—not the wide plaza that stretches in front of the Wall today—was a plain table, with a few Sten guns on it! Uniformed paratroopers wrapped in praying shawls were clinging so tightly to the Wall that it seemed impossible to separate them from it—they and the Wall were one. These heroes, who only a few hours before had fought furiously for the liberation of Jerusalem, who had seen their comrades fall for Jerusalem's sake, went up to the Wall. They wept and wrapped themselves in praying shawls. I, too, took a sheet of paper, wrote the word "Shalom" on it and put it into a cranny of the Wall.

I shall never forget the picture of the boys by the Wall. It is one of the greatest moments of my life. While I stood there, a soldier who probably did not recognize me put his arms around me and his head on my shoulder. I felt greatly blessed that at that moment a young lad whom I did not know chose me to be a mother to him when he felt the need to weep on the shoulder of someone close and dear.

Recently, I had the privilege together with all of you to stand before the Wall in a tragic hour of our people's history to express solidarity with the men and women who were there to protest what was happening to the Jews in the Soviet Union. This was a grave occasion, but also a glorious one, for a great miracle had taken place. For almost sixty years the Russian Jewish community endured the full weight of a mighty power. The whole force of a regime of unrestrained cruelty was brought to bear on Russian Jewry to sever it from its past and present and to deprive it of any hope of sharing in the future of the Jewish people. Nevertheless, today not only Jews from the free world and other diasporas are standing at the Wall. The Soviet Jews themselves, each of whom suffered greatly in this struggle, are standing on the soil of the homeland, in Jerusalem, and are demanding freedom for the comrades they left behind.

The day before yesterday, when all the members of the Cabinet went to the Wall, I saw a handsome boy of twenty or twenty-one who had come from Kovno. "Did you come with your family?" I asked him. "Yes, with my family." "How long did it take before they let you leave?" "Only a year," he said. "But," he added, "in that year I spent some time in prison."

Despite hardship and peril, for we know what has been happening in the Soviet Union, the Russian Jews do not give up. Even under that regime, young Jews, old men and whole families venture to declare openly: "We are Jews, part of our people; our people has a homeland; it is our homeland. Let us go!"

The boy from Kovno told me: "I was one of those who took part in a sit-down strike at the building of the Presidium of the Supreme Soviet. It's easy to get in, but rather complicated to get out." But this youth not only got out of the building—he got out of the Soviet Union, and he is here. When I visited the hunger strikers at the Wall a few months ago, I saw a woman who was weeping for her sons and her daughter who had remained in Russia. But on the occasion I am describing she was again at the Wall, this time with her three sons and her daughter; they too had arrived.

I have no illusions; the Soviet Jews will undergo many trials, but they are no longer suffering like men who have been condemned and have accepted the verdict; they are suffering like people who have rebelled against injustice and are prepared to fight. At last we are privileged to see them in our midst.

Fifty years is a long time; yet to have been able to witness these events it was worth living through these fifty years. Perhaps I may be permitted to mention that I have also had one other privilege: It was in Jerusalem that my children, my son and daughter, were born; my grandchildren present here, are the second generation of my family born in Israel. I am happy that my grandchildren are sitting here. Perhaps they will remember this occasion, not because of what was said here about their grandmother, but because they will be able to tell their children and their grandchildren that once, in Jerusalem, the capital of Israel, they were present at a ceremony when the freedom of the city was awarded, not to their grandmother, but to a Prime Minister of Israel, the head of a Jewish state. Fortunate we who live in that state!

26. My Life Has Been Blessed

On accepting the Stephen Wise Award of the American Jewish Congress. (In English, July 25, 1959)

Fifty-four years ago, together with other children of my age, I stood on the steps of a house in Kiev and watched my father and other fathers hammering planks across the doors of our homes for fear of pogroms that were expected in our town. Then I did not understand exactly what was happening around us; all the children were silent. The only sound was the knocking of hammers. We felt with the deep instinct of children that something dreadful and serious was taking place. As I recall that day, I ask: If it has been given in one lifetime to go all the way from the sound of that hammer in Kiev to life in the state of Israel—where though we have no complete security, we have the assurance that we are not at the mercy of pogroms and that, if anyone strikes at us, we have the power to defend our children—how much more can a Jew ask? So many millions of Jews throughout the ages—and millions before our very eyes—were not able to defend themselves like us.

My next memory is of Pinsk, when at the age of six or seven I used to climb stealthily onto the kitchen stove (those who come from Russia know those old stoves); from this hiding place I used to spy on what was going on in the little room where my mother lived with her three daughters. By then my father was already in America. My older sister, aged sixteen, would be hatching secret conspiracies with a group of boys and girls of her age. She would walk about the room on the watch for police who might burst in. These boys and girls, like so many others in Russia, used to meet to plan the overthrow of the czarist regime so as to usher in a free and humane system of government. To this day no one has been a greater influence for good in my life than this sister of mine. Then I did not understand the mysterious meetings, but I felt that Mother was nervous, and I sensed that I was witnessing something serious and important. It has been my happy fortune to go all the way from that small room in a despotic land to life in the state of Israel, where there are a great workers' movement, humane workers' enterprises, agricultural settlements, and the cooperatives of the kibbutz and the moshav. If a Jewish woman who was a child in that little room lives to be blessed with a daughter and grandchildren living in a kibbutz under a system that cannot be surpassed for equality and respect for human dignity, what more can she desire?

In my youth I worked in the kibbutz of Merhavia. I remember that Merhavia was then situated between two Arab villages, and one of the first things my comrades told me was that I should not go out into the yard in a white dress at night because a white dress could be seen from a distance in the dark and made a good target.

In Merhavia in 1921 they did not believe that a "soft" American girl would prove a serious worker. Yet these same skeptical comrades, after a trial period, pronounced me a good worker, both in the poultry yard and in planting trees on the hill facing Merhavia (the forest was on rocky ground, and digging holes on that hill was no simple matter). I thought then and I still think Merhavia's acceptance of me as a full-fledged member of the kibbutz was one of the most satisfactory achievements of my life. I am sorry to this day that I must speak of life in the kibbutz as of something in the past. Already in youth I became convinced that the way of the kibbutz was the right way; it was the solution for the problem of how men should live most fruitfully, even though the idea was hard to carry out and only a few people believed in it. What more can one expect to have in Israel, if in the course of the thirty-six years I have been privileged to live in this country I have seen this dream become a reality to a degree greater than anyone would have imagined?

I remember the grave decisions that had to be taken in the clash between the illusion that we would be able to realize our vision of Jewish independence by means of negotiations, appeals, and protests and the recognition that we had no choice but to take our fate into our own hands and be ready to pay a very heavy price to prove that we would not accept the kind of "justice" under which might was right and the weak were to be left at the mercy of the strong. In the days of our great struggle, I said, "Let us fight." I do not boast that I am fearless —I am very far from being fearless. We were faced with a choice between two fears—the fear of yielding to a regime that was ready to sacrifice us and the fear of fighting for our just cause. In fear and trembling I chose my path. And indeed we paid dearly. But if a Jewish woman who saw shiploads of Jews, survivors of the extermination camps, come to the shores of Palestine only to be turned back, is now privileged to live in the state of Israel to which nearly a million Jews have come in a ceaseless stream—men, women, and children who enter not on sufferance but in the knowledge that they are coming home— for what more can she ask?

And what more can any Jewish woman desire, if she had the privilege to be the first one to reach Soviet Jewry, which for decades had been completely cut off from all contact with us? Many of us in our hearts sometimes doubted whether Russian Jews would find the infinite strength to go on caring about what we were doing in Israel or as long as need be until the link between us could be forged anew. Whoever has heard the words "Next year in Jerusalem" from the lips of those Jews, in the synagogue and during the Day of Atonement prayers— even if he lives to be a hundred and devotes all his strength and energy to the land and the people of Israel—will remain a debtor forever.

Through the years I learned in our movement how to go on living here, with our Arab neighbors attacking us periodically, when often not one road in the country was safe; we learned how to hold out against these neighbors of ours and at the same time not to hate them, but to long truly for the day when they would take our hand outstretched in peace and we would be able to build together a happy life for this whole region. To go on living like this is a great art and a valuable achievement. It is not written down in any books. I learned it from our way of life as I lived it here, from the earnest longing for peace of our people, dwelling in Zion. This people is prepared to forgive and forget for the sake of attaining the tranquillity in which both we and our neighbors would be able to work creatively. What more can I demand, after being privileged to live among a people such as this?

Perhaps you will think it just pretense—but believe me, on no day of my life have I said to myself in a mood of self-satisfaction, "Well, today I've done something for the people of Israel, the state of Israel." I have always been aware that I have been boundlessly blessed by the experiences granted me. Perhaps it was the merits of my forebears that earned me this privilege: My father's father was conscripted into the Russian Army at the age of twelve and was forced to violate Jewish religious commandments in the Army; for the rest of his life after he returned—so my father used to tell me, for I never knew this grandfather—he used to sleep on a wooden bench with a stone instead of a pillow, in order to atone for the transgressions he had committed under duress.

For myself, after all that I have known, I desire only one thing more: to live only as long as I can live a full life in the state of Israel and never to lose the feeling that it is I who am indebted for what has been given me.

PLAIN TALK

Excerpts from interviews in Hebrew and English.

ON BEING A WOMAN

All my adult life I have worked among men, and they have treated me on my merits. I never knew a man who gave in to an argument of mine because I was a woman—except one, my husband—and they had the open-mindedness and the manliness to accept my idea if they thought it was right. I always tried to reciprocate—I didn't expect privileges because I was a woman, and if the majority was against me, I accepted it, even if I knew it was a man's idea . . . and wrong.

I think women often get not so much an unfair deal as an illogical one. Once in the Cabinet we had to deal with the fact that there had been an outbreak of assaults on women at night. One minister (a member of an extreme religious party) suggested a curfew. Women should stay at home after dark. I said: "But it's the men who are attacking the women. If there's to be a curfew, let the men stay at home, not the women."

ON ZIONISM

Those who talk about returning are recent arrivals. An old worker is full of inspiration and faith. I say that as long as those who created the little that is here are here, I cannot leave, and you must come. I would not say this if I did not know that you are ready to work hard. True, even hard work is hard to find, but I have no doubt that you will find something. Of course, this is not America, and one may have to suffer a lot economically. There may even be pogroms again, but if one wants one's own land, and if one wants it with one's whole heart, one must be ready for this. When you come, I am sure we will be able to plan. Perhaps you will come with us to Merhavia. Get ready. There is nothing to wait for. (From a letter, August 24, 1921)

There is no Zionism except the rescue of Jews. (1943)

The step in my life I'm most proud and happy about is my decision to come to Palestine when I did. Sometimes when I go to the United States, when I go to my hometown, Milwaukee, I meet my friends who were with me from the early years. We had done many things together. We were in the Labor Zionist party together, we demonstrated against Jewish mistreatment during World War I and had all kinds of plans, but they remained in the United States. My old friends are very well off and their children are economically much better off than my children, yet I feel a little bit sorry for them. So if I did anything that I can say with 100 percent assurance that it was right for me it was that decision in my youth. (1969)

If the Second Aliyah had accepted the notion that we were all going to be owners of orange groves, stores, and factories, while others worked for us, we would never have achieved independence. We would have had no moral title to a land built by others.

With the introduction of technology, physical labor becomes less necessary and attractive. But some things have to be done with your own hands. You have to soil your hands; I would not like to see all of us with university degrees while others do the dirty work. This would vitally injure our society. This is not Zionism. (*Jerusalem Post*, April 20, 1970)

Zionism and pessimism are not compatible.

ON PEACE

Peace will come when the Arabs will love their children more than they hate us. (National Press Club, Washington, 1957)

When peace comes we will perhaps in time be able to forgive the Arabs for killing our sons, but it will be harder for us to forgive them for having forced us to kill their sons. (Press conference in London, 1969)

Israel wants direct talks with the Arabs because you can't make peace underground.

Nasser must realize that peace is not a luxury. It is something that his children, the children of the Nile Valley, need as much as we do.

When people ask me if I am not afraid that because of Israel's need for defense, the country may become militaristic, I can only answer that I don't want a fine, liberal, anticolonial, antimilitaristic *dead* Jewish people.

I want my grandchildren to live in an Israel that is part and parcel of this entire area, but I don't want them to live in an Israel that will always be complimented as the only democratic state here, the only developed state. I want Israel to be part of a highly developed culturally advanced Middle East with much cooperation between its peoples. Each people maintaining its individual characteristics and yet a region that lives together. Above all, I hope that Israel will become the ideal, just society of which we dreamed. (1970)

Index